PARTICULAR PONDERING(S)

Particular Pondering(s)
Copyright © 2020
Wayne Berry

Cover concept and design by David Warren.

All rights reserved. No part of this book may be reproduced, stored in a retrieval system, or transmitted in any form or by any means—electronic, mechanical, photocopy, recording or otherwise—without the prior written permission of the publisher. The only exception is brief quotations for review purposes.

Published by WordCrafts Press
Cody, Wyoming 82414
www.wordcrafts.net

Particular Pondering(s)

Essays: Relevant & Random

WAYNE BERRY

WordCrafts

Unless otherwise noted all Scripture quotations are taken from the New American Standard Bible ® (NASB), Copyright © 1960, 1962, 1963, 1968, 1971, 1972, 1973, 1975, 1977, 1995 by The Lockman Foundation. Used by permission. www.Lockman.org

Scripture quotations marked (ESV) are from the ESV® Bible (The Holy Bible, English Standard Version®), copyright © 2001 by Crossway, a publishing ministry of Good News Publishers. Used by permission. All rights reserved.

Scripture quotations marked (MSG) taken from THE MESSAGE. Copyright © by Eugene H. Peterson 1993, 1994, 1995, 1996, 2000, 2001, 2002. Used by permission of NavPress. All rights reserved. Represented by Tyndale House Publishers, Inc.

Scripture quotations marked (Phillips) are fromThe New Testament in Modern English by J.B Phillips copyright © 1960, 1972 J. B. Phillips. Administered by The Archbishops' Council of the Church of England. Used by Permission.

Scripture quotations marked (CEV) are from the Contemporary English Version, copyright © 1991, 1992, 1995 by American Bible Society. Used by Permission.

Scripture quotations marked (LEB) are from the Lexham English Bible. Copyright 2012 Logos Bible Software. Lexham is a registered trademark of Logos Bible Software.

Scripture quotations marked (MEV) are taken from the Modern English Version. Copyright © 2014 by Military Bible Association. Used by permission. All rights reserved.

Scripture quotations marked (NIV) are taken from THE HOLY BIBLE, NEW INTERNATIONAL VERSION®, NIV® Copyright © 1973, 1978, 1984, 2011 by Biblica, Inc.™ Used by permission. All rights reserved worldwide.

Scripture quotations marked TPT are from TPT®. Copyright © 2017, 2018 by Passion & Fire Ministries, Inc. Used by permission. All rights reserved. ThePassionTranslation.com.

Scripture quotations marked (JUB) are from The Jubilee Bible 2000 (From the Scriptures of the Reformation) Copyright © 2013, 2020 Translated and Edited by Russell M. Stendal May. Used by permission.

Scripture quotations marked (GOD'S WORD) are taken from GOD'S WORD TRANSLATION. GOD'S WORD is a copyrighted work of God's Word to the Nations. Quotations are used by permission. Copyright 1995 by God's Word to the Nations. All rights reserved.

Scripture quotations marked (CSB) are been taken from the Christian Standard Bible®, Copyright © 2017 by Holman Bible Publishers. Used by permission. Christian Standard Bible•, and CSB® are federally registered trademarks of Holman Bible Publishers.

Scripture quotations marked (KJV) taken from the King James Version of the Bible, public domain.

Scipture quotations marked (NHEB) taken from the New Heart English Bible, public domain.

Scripture quotations marked (MOF) are from the James Moffatt, A New Translation of the Bible, Containing the Old and New Testaments. New York: Doran, 1926. Revised edition, New York and London: Harper and Brothers, 1935. Reprinted, Grand Rapids: Kregel, 1995.

Ponder:

(O.T.) To roll flat (as in preparing a roadway); to cause to revolve; to weigh out mentally. (N.T.) To combine together or consider in a unified manner. (From *Strong's Concordance*)

Essay:

NOUN: a short piece of writing on a particular subject
    synonyms: article, piece of writing, composition, study, paper, dissertation
  formal: an attempt or effort; "a misjudged essay"
    synonyms: attempt, effort, endeavor, try, venture, trial, experiment, undertaking
VERB: attempt or try; "essay a smile"
    synonyms: attempt, make an attempt at, try, strive, aim, venture, endeavor, seek

Author's Note

The content of this book may not be of interest to anyone, really. But I am making it potentially available to everyone. Why? Because I can. These are my thoughts, insights, and observations—my ongoing pondering(s). So, I'm—just sayin'.

Since the creative process and the expenses necessary to go from inception to publication and then on to printing has been mine to sort through—and to cover—I can make this work accessible to all those who are interested and willing to pay the purchase price, receive it as a gift, or find it in their lap. A Divine happenstance of a sort perhaps.

My personal goal for this project is a very simple one. I've purposed to gather up my musings into this manuscript, wrap a cover 'round it, and lift it up before the Lord as an offering of *worship. Once the wind of the Spirit catches it, wherever it's carried thereafter will be completely up to the Lord. (Jn. 3:8 and Col. 3:17)

Worship is obedient service manifesting through self-sacrifice.

"As a man thinketh in his heart, so is he..."
~Pro. 23:7 (KJV)

DEDICATIONS

To Jean, my wife of 40+ years, for her faithful covenant keeping as my life-partner. (Gen. 2:24 and Pro. 18:22)

To Claudia for her kingdom comradeship. A worship warrior who's lived her life on the front lines of the battlefield. (Isa. 30:31-32)

To Ximena for her love of words, her patience toward me as proof reader for all three of my manuscripts, and her ongoing encouragement to those who pursue the will and ways of God's kingdom. (Mt. 6:33)

To Mike and Paula for their work(s) of faith, labor(s) of love, and steadfastness of hope. (1 Thess. 1:2-4)

And to each and every "teaching Levite" that knows who they are and what their calling is. You are not carrying your burden alone dear cohorts. (2 Chron. 35:2-4)

*"If I had been born just 10 years sooner, I know where I would be
Workin' on my novel for Random House, and livin' off my poetry
But one way or other, my stars got crossed
And I wound up here somehow
I'd be better off a beatnik, better off a beatnik
I'd be better off a beatnik than what I am now"*

(From: "Better Off A Beatnik"
W. Berry & George S. Clinton / See & Say Songs, BMI)

Contents

Part 1

Berry's Blognessisms 1
World Of Wonders 2
Ears To Hear 6
Wind Blown Worship 8
Wind Blown Worship 12
A Father's Day Declaration 15
Repentant Worship 22
The Not-So-Constant Gardener 30
A Good Gift 34
Morning Has Broken 38
Entering In 40
The Ultimate Worship Warrior 44
Generational Networking 47
Salvation & Sanctification 51
The Ministry Of Obscurity 53
Why Worship 55
God's Got You Covered 58
Pondering Prayer 60

Part 2

Revelant & Random 62
Corporate Unity & Enthroning God 63
Up There, Down Here 70
Past-Tense Positioning 72
Reconciliation & Ambassadorship 74

SMALL UP YOURSELF 76
FEELIN' GROOVY 77
COMPUTE THIS 78
OR RE-PONDERING 80
JESUS SAID 82
DESCRIPTION AND TITLE 84
FAITH 85
GIFTED AND REQUESTED 87
BROKENNESS OR BREAKTHROUGH 88
DIVINE TECH SUPPORT 91
PROFIT AND LOSS 92
PURPOSED-PRO-ACTIVITY 94
TWO KINDS OF HOPE 95
FAITH AND/OR TRUST 97
INTERNAL INTAKE AND SPIRITUAL HEALTH 99
KINGDOM PONDERING(S) 101
WORD UP 103
KINGDOM CONSIDERATIONS 104
ANOTHER KINGDOM PONDERING 106
THE HUMAN CONDITION 108
LISTENING FOR SILENCE 110
LIFE AND LIFESTYLE 111
THE RX FOR CURING NATIONALIZED RELIGION(S) 112
ON PROSE 113
LIVING IN CRAZY-DAZE 114
A BOOMER'S POV 115
CHANNELING GRACE 116
KINGDOM STUFF 118
GENERATIONAL UNITY 119
PONDERING WORSHIP 122
PONDERING POWER 124

GENERATIONAL LINKAGE 126
WINE AND WINESKINS 130
THY KINGDOM COME, THY WILL BE DONE 133
A NEW YEAR TESTIMONAL 135
THE GOODNESS AND GRACE OF OUR FATHER 137
20/20 VISION 139
WORSHIP 140
WORD PICTURES 142
PROPHETIC FULFILLMENT 143
REPENTANCE 145
CONSIDERING BLESSEDNESS 147
ON EARTH AS IT IS IN HEAVEN 149
REDEMPTIVE COMPONENTS 151
FOR THOSE OVER 40 152
TREE / ACORN 153
ON WORSHIP LEADERSHIP 156
TICK-TOCK 157
THINGS ABOVE 159
A PHASES PHRASE 162
HUMILITY AND EXALTATION 163
SOJOURNERS UPDATE 166
LIGHT VS. DARKNESS 168
PONDERING GRACE 175
THEOLOGICAL ADJUSTMENTS 176
SOVEREIGNTY 177
PROCESSING "THE PRESENCE" 180
TONGUE TROUBLES 202
HOPE 205
PONDERING CIRCUMSTANCE 209
DIVINE HAPPENSTANCE 211
WHY HUMANS? 213

Faith 218
Listening To Language 220
Being And Doing 221
Kingdom Considerations 222
Thy Kingdom Come 225
Receiving And Giving 227
Approximated Anecdotal Axiom 230
Computing The Kingdom 231
The Process Of Processing 233
Performance Vs. Performance 235
The Security Of Sanctuary Discovery 238
Never Lose Your Song 245
The Shape Of Destiny 252
Seed Sowing 256
Chattering(S) 261
Joseph's Journey: 267
Kingdom Citizenship Vs. Nationalized Christianity 278
Pondering Trust 296
The Process Of Consecration 297
Content And Context 306
Spiritual Recalibration 308
Reaping And Sowing 313
To My Spiritual Cohorts 315
Pastor To Pasture 316
Transcending Tribalism 318
Still Standing 324
Observational Implications 329
Humbled Prayer 331
Combating The Global Pandemic Of Loneliness 334
A Place To Stand 336
Kingdom Dynamics 338

Sorry Vs. Forgiveness 339
Hope For Hope 340
Plans & Purposes 342
The Principle Of Biblical Humaliation 344
Worship In Specific 346
Scriptural Obedience 347
An Eternal Perspective In A Temporal World 350
Previous Projects 353

PART I
BERRY'S BLOGNESSISMS
(An Archived Array)

The following section contains blogged data (remember blogs?) drafted over a period of 18 months or thereabouts from back in the daze. I've included them here for two reasons:

To make them available for anyone who may come across them and choose to read them.

Because this is my book and I can include pretty much anything I want to.

> *"One of the few things I know about writing is this: spend it all, shoot it, play it, lose it, all, right away, every time. Do not hoard what seems good for a later place in the book, or for another book; give it, give it all, give it now... Something more will arise for later, something better. These things fill from behind, from beneath, like well water. Similarly, the impulse to keep to yourself what you have learned is not only shameful, it is destructive. Anything you do not give freely and abundantly becomes lost to you. You open your safe and find ashes."*
> ~Annie Dillard

Wednesday, March 18, 2009
WORLD OF WONDERS

God is Creator of everything! That of course includes all of life on this planet, the heavens above us, and the ever-expanding universe as well. Through His sovereign and endless creativity, He has provided the seasons as a context for all of life to express praise and adoration for this *world of wonders*. For those who have the spiritual eyes to see it—the earth really is filled with His glory.

There is a passage in God's Word that addresses this in a grand way. In Romans 1:20 Paul makes a statement as to what could perhaps be considered the bedrock of kingdom evangelism. He states that there are things most wondrously infused into the DNA of earth which can, or should, serve as keys to unlocking the door leading to the Gospel, and then on to confession, repentance, conversion, and covenant relationship, followed by a life of consecration as servant-stewards unto the Lord.

> *"The basic reality of God is plain enough. Open your eyes and there it is! By taking a long and thoughtful look at what God has created, people have always been able to see what their eyes*

as such can't see: eternal power, for instance, and the mystery of his divine being. So nobody has a good excuse."

~Rom. 1:20 (MSG)

I've recently returned with a team of my kingdom comrades from a ministry trip to South Africa. The huge expanse of the continent is truly overwhelming to experience first hand. Everything is, well, just bigger there! The immensity of the clouds, the seemingly endless vistas from the mountain tops, the visual and visceral perspective of time and space standing in the deserts—and of course the drive time from wherever you may be to wherever you're headed next—all come together in a way that brings you to your knees, while at the same time seeming to raise your heart to higher levels of praise and deeper levels of worship for God's benevolent handiwork.

All that our eyes can behold in the nature of this earth is what Scripture calls the "fringes of His ways."

"He spreads the skies over unformed space, hangs the earth out in empty space. He pours water into cumulus cloud-bags and the bags don't burst. He makes the moon wax and wane, putting it through its phases. He draws the horizon out over the ocean, sets a boundary between light and darkness. Thunder crashes and rumbles in the skies. Listen! It's God raising his voice! By his power he stills sea storms, by his wisdom he tames sea monsters. With one breath he clears the sky, with one finger he crushes the sea serpent. And this is only the beginning, A mere whisper of his rule. Whatever would we do if he really raised his voice!"

~Job 26:7-14 (MSG)

PARTICULAR PONDERING(S)

Here in America, as we enter into the season of spring with its new growth, new promise, and new life coming up all around us it's a very good time to renew your vision of God's unfolding kingdom. This should be a time of thankfulness for the days that the Lord is giving us.

Don't be fooled or misled by the news you hear coming at you from every direction. Birth, new birth, is taking place. There are healings, mighty acts of deliverance, divine encounters, and new converts being added to the kingdom daily. God releases new mercy with each new sunrise. Just keep looking till it begins to come into focus. And if the glasses you're viewing your life through don't seem to be working well anymore, perhaps you just need some new lenses.

"The heavens are declaring the righteousness of the Lord."
~Ps. 50:6

INVISIBLE GOD

I give you praise, O Great Invisible God
For the moon in the space of a dark night
For the smile on a face in the sunlight
I give you praise, O Great Invisible God
For the sound of the storm on the window
For the morning adorned with a new snow
For the tears on the face of the old man
Made clean by the grace of the good Lamb

And oh, I long to see your face, Invisible, Invisible God
All the works that you have made are clearly seen and plain as day
So mighty and tender. O Lord, let me remember

WORLD OF WONDERS

That I see you everywhere Invisible God
In the seed that descends to the old earth
And arises again with a new birth
In the sinner who sinks in the river and emerges again, delivered

And oh, I long to see your face, Invisible, Invisible God
All the works that you have made are clearly seen and plain as day
So mighty and tender. O Lord, let me remember
Your power eternal, your nature divine
All creation tells the tale that Love is real and so alive
I feel you, I hear you, Great God Unseen I see you
In the long, cold death that the winter brings
And the sweet resurrection spring.

-*Invisible God*
from *Resurrection Letters Vol. 2*
by Andrew Peterson
used by permission

Posted by WORSHIP ARTS at 6:58 PM

Friday, April 24, 2009
EARS TO HEAR
(The Sound of Otherness)

Previously I commented about *songs of deliverance* (Ps. 32:7) and I asked you if you were able to hear them surrounding you. This business of hearing things supernatural can be a very tricky thing to try and accomplish.

Hearing spiritual things requires spiritual ears tuned to frequencies which are outside—above and beyond—our earthly senses. To be open for and sensitive to such transcendent sonic-ness we have to first desire to hear the *otherness* coming forth from God's eternal kingdom. Then we have to begin to understand that such hearing as that doesn't happen through casual contact. Relationship is required in order for the lines of communication to be strung into place. For without a connecting point to *things above* (Col. 3:1-3) our reception can only be random at best. And, regardless of the increasingly popular post-modern-mindset, randomness isn't necessarily the best way to move thorough one's life and times. That however is a subject for another blog down the road a ways—perhaps.

For now—how's your link to the Trinity? Dropped any calls lately?

EARS TO HEAR

A pondering: In Jn. 12, verses 28, 29 we are told how the sounds of heaven can be received—or not. Verse 28 says that "a voice out of heaven" spoke. Verse 29 gives us two examples of how such a sound as that can be processed. One group of bystanders responded by stating "that it had thundered." The other respondents said that "an angel had spoken." If you'll allow me just a little flex room with this passage please, I think there could well have been a third group present at that moment of "divine encounter" who missed it all together. That group would have been comprised of those who heard nothing at all. No thunder. No angels. No nothing. Personal experience has taught me that such people are still among us today. Just look around. There are folks everywhere who never hear or see any evidence of God's presence, power or purpose on the earth or in the heavens above (see Rom. 1:20). Sad but true.

When the voice of the Lord speaks, which group are you in? As *songs of deliverance* are being sung around you, you may or may not be aware of them. That all depends on how receptive you are to things eternal. And, that's a "where your treasure is" sort of thing (Luke 12:22-34).

Can you hear Him now? Just checking.

Posted by WORSHIP ARTS at 10:48 AM

Monday, June 1, 2009
WIND BLOWN WORSHIP
(Part #1)

"Blowing toward the south, then turning toward the north, the wind continues swirling along; and on its circular courses the wind returns."

~Ecc. 1:6

I'm continuing with thoughts from my previous blog focused on hearing things related to God's kingdom which come at us from outside of our normal, everyday lives. I want to share a story with you. It concerns an event that deeply impacted my life, my perceptions about living, and my future/destiny. In fact the term "life-changing" is appropriate for what I have to share.

The story begins in late September of 2004 standing in the middle of nowhere in Kenya, Africa. I was returning with a short-term mission team from a region located in the very shadow of Mt. Kilimanjaro. We had spent 10 days or so building two church structures for the Maasai tribespeople who had converted to Christianity. After finishing and dedicating (consecrating) both buildings, we started our journey out of the bush toward a paved highway that would take us back to Nairobi. Driving along roads that really weren't roads at all, one of our Land Rovers broke down. Fortunately our team guide had the know-how and the tools needed to make the necessary repairs. However, doing so was going to take a while. So, we all piled out of our vehicles and purposed to make the most of our time until things got sorted out.

Waiting patiently for circumstances to change is a major part of the African lifestyle. It's in the DNA of those on the continent. If you go there you will find that out for yourself.

Here's what happened:

During our time together as a team we had learned that we weren't to walk too far away from the others when we were out in the bush. Things can get dangerous in such an environment, so staying within eyesight of each other is pretty important. Our team leader had released us to roam the area near the vehicles, instructing us to stay close. We began to amble around in groups of twos and threes. A few of us went off on our own a brief distance away. I had walked away by myself to take care of nature's call behind a couple of scrub trees, when something very unusual began to occur as I turned to head back facing into the breeze that was rising up out of the valley which opened up just below us.

As I turned I began to hear what sounded like music. More specifically it sounded like singing. To be exact it sounded like children singing. And to fine-tune that even further, I heard children singing what seemed to me like worship. The *sound* was very brief—two or three seconds at the most—but I know worship when I hear it. It's a "deep calls to deep" thing (Ps. 42:7).

What I heard stunned me. How could this be happening? We were in the middle of nowhere, so how could there be singing? Where would it come from? And how could it be *kids'* voices?

As I continued to turn my face directly toward the wind, the sound disappeared. As soon as it was there, it was gone. I stopped in my tracks and began to try and figure out what was taking place. I turned my head ever so slightly to re-center myself, and when I did the wind shifted and blew more directly into my ear again instead of straight into my face. When that happened the sound returned. This time it was as clear as a bell, but not very loud. Got the picture? So, now I'm getting excited because my brain, and my senses, are starting to catch up with my spirit. I turned my face directly back into the wind and the sound disappeared again.

Now I was on to something that was beyond my immediate comprehension. As I turned my head away from the wind blowing at me directly, the air current blew into my ear again instead of into my face. Then what was happening hit me like a bolt of lightning. What I was hearing was on the wind—or in the wind. The sound was coming from somewhere as yet to be determined, and it was being carried on/by the wind itself. In fact, it couldn't be detected unless my ear was turned exactly the right way in order to catch the sound as it blew in my direction. In other words—*without being positioned properly I couldn't hear the singing at all.* Saints, that'll preach!

I glanced back up the ridge to see if any of the others from the team knew what I was experiencing. Not a clue—they had heard nothing. They weren't positioned (tuned in) to it at all.

I was having a divine appointment and people within earshot of me had no idea!

Selah…pause and consider.

Once I realized what kind of *moment* I was in, I locked into the sound like a laser-tracking beam. I began to move toward it. But every time I turned directly into the wind I lost the singing. I could only stay on track by turning my head ever so slightly every few steps. That way the wind carried the sound into my ear, and I could adjust my path of pursuit accordingly. My heart was pounding, and my soul was caught up in the dynamics of what was taking place. I had to know where the singing was coming from and who was creating it. So up toward the top of the ridge I ran yelling like a crazy man for the others to join me. But the angle I was moving in was taking me away from those on the team, and the wind was carrying the sound of my voice—along with the sound of the singing—away from my comrades.

The only person near enough to really hear me was a sister from our worship choir back in our home church. As I motioned for her to meet me at the top of the ridge she began to head in that direction. She had no idea what was waiting up at the crest—and neither did I.

To be continued…

WIND BLOWN WORSHIP
(Part #2)

"Blowing toward the south, then turning toward the north, the wind continues swirling along; and on its circular courses the wind returns."

~Ecc. 1:6

Continued from my last posting...

As Patti and I topped the rise of the ridge we saw the valley opening up below us and beyond us toward a small mountain range in the distance. The valley wasn't very deep, but it was fairly wide and long. On the edge nearest us, as we looked down, we could see a dry river bed which continued out and away from where we stood. At the base of the ridge just below us we saw something besides land and space. There was what appeared to be a sort of fort made from slender tree trunks which had been stripped clean of their bark. The fort was constructed in a rectangular shape and open to the sky. It had just four walls of wood with no ceiling. As we stood there trying to figure out what it was, suddenly everything locked into place in one profoundly amazing moment. The wind off the valley floor picked up and began to rise up the side of the ridge toward where we were positioned looking downward. And what it carried up to us was now hitting us square in our faces. It was the sound of children singing at the top of their voices. It was such a precious and passionate sound. Such beauty and wonder in such a dry and barren place. This *no place* had become a high and holy place *in the middle of nowhere.*

I turned toward Patti who up until that moment had no idea of why I had called her to join me there. She hadn't heard a sound till it rose up on the wind and overwhelmed her. I looked at her with tears in my eyes, matched by her own, and I said, "Patti, it's a school, and the kids are singing praise songs!" There under the open and expansive African sky, the Holy Ghost fell big time, and my sister and I were overcome by the sound, tears, smiles and joy of it all.

In the very next instant one side of the fort opened up where a doorway was positioned, and all the kids ran out of their classroom, made a turn away from us, and moved out beyond and down into the dry riverbed laughing, jumping and having a grand time of it. I looked at Patti through more tears, and I said, "It's recess."

We both began to laugh out loud as we thanked God for His precious gift to us. As we stood there taking it all in, the Holy Ghost spoke to me with a word of revelation. He said, "No place, is some place, to somebody." At that moment my global perspective exploded. My view of humanity, the nations, and God's ever-expanding kingdom took on entirely new dimensions. My understanding of His omnipresence had been blown totally off the charts. I was awestruck!

There's much more to this story than I've presented here. It continues to impact my life and ministry almost daily. But it's my understanding that blogs work best if they remain brief. So, I'll end with this:

God's *otherness* is a very real thing to encounter. The eternal dynamics of His kingdom—the ebb and flow—are constantly at work. We are "compassed about" (Ps. 32:7 / KJV) by the sights and sounds of His Divine Presence in truly supernatural ways.

Allow the Spirit of the Lord to open up your senses, your soul, and your very being to the glory and wonder of it all.

And may His kingdom come (manifest) on earth as it is in heaven.

Let me mention one last thing to those of you who lead congregations in corporate worship on a regular basis. Please be encouraged by this *Fact!* Worship, heart-felt, soul-engaged, pure, honest, and undefiled worship is being released all over this earth every moment of every day—24/7/365. God has purposed and ordained it to be that way (Ps. 150:6 / Luke 19:40). But the thing is, we're not always standing in the right spot, at the right moment, with our heads turned just the right way to be able to hear it. Nonetheless, it is there. I can personally testify to the fact that there is worship on the wind coming from people in places that you'd never imagine.

> *"All of heaven's waiting*
> *All the earth expecting*
> *Sons, daughters, arise*
> *Singing songs of freedom*
> *Words of healing*
> *One voice, wind blown worship"*
>
> From: *Hallelujah* / By: Denise Graves
> used by permission
> Posted by WORSHIP ARTS at 6:32 AM

Saturday, June 13, 2009
A FATHER'S DAY DECLARATION
I WILL NOT RUN

My great-grandfather was an angry man, he abused his family
He passed along that heritage, through the roots of our family tree
His children turned against him, and they drove him from his home
Never knowing where he ended up, or if he died alone

My grandfather was an honest man, he tried to live what's right
But somewhere in the darkness, he fell without a fight
He took his sons, and dignity, and threw them in his truck
And he drove off in the shadows tryin' to break his string of luck

I will not run, I will not run
By God's grace, I'll stand and face
Each new day as it comes
I will not run, I will not run
The family curse has been reversed
The healing has begun
And I will not run

My father was a godly man, of that there is no doubt

PARTICULAR PONDERING(S)

He told me once when he was young, he tried taking the wrong way out
But his love for God, and mom, and me, was stronger than his fear
So Jesus Christ was honored through the life dad lived down here

I will not run, I will not run, by God's grace
I'll stand and face, each new day as it comes
I will not run, I will not run
The family curse has been reversed
Now there's a blessing for my son
For I will not run

(By: W. Berry / See & Say Songs, BMI)

I sang that song at church on Father's Day Sunday for several years. I stopped singing it because I felt the Holy Ghost saying I should lay it aside for a while. However it has been stirring around in my spirit the last several weeks so perhaps the time has come for it to be repristinated.

I'm told that the more personal a blog can be the better—more interesting—it is for the reader. I don't know if I can get any more personal than opening up some of my family history to you. So, here goes...

The first verse above is about my great-grandfather on my dad's side of the family. The story that my grandmother told to me works itself out like this:

He was a farmer in the South sometime during the first half of the 1800's or thereabouts. He began his family—my family—by kidnapping a young Cherokee maiden. He somehow managed to elude the young warriors from her tribe that tried to track him down, intent on killing him, and rescuing her. They were married (?) and during their life together had eight to 10 children. As the children grew up he became more and more violent—especially toward his wife, my great-grandmother. One day he beat her and knocked her to the ground. She was pregnant at the time. He picked up a stick of firewood and in his rage he yelled out that he was "gonna beat that baby out of you!" His sons by then were apparently old enough and strong enough and angry enough to have reached their breaking point. They came to their mother's defense and chased him off at gun point and told him that if they ever saw him again they would shoot him. A sorry state of affairs to be sure. After that dreadful event took place no one in the family ever saw or heard from him again. So the subject matter of that opening verse is a painfully sad, but true, story.

The second verse takes place a generation later and involves my grandfather on my mother's side. If you thought verse one was intense then consider this:

My mother's mother died when she was only three. Her father remarried not long afterward, having two teenage sons and a baby daughter to raise. The woman he married had been married twice before. Both husbands had died under "mysterious circumstances." The gossip in the community was that she had killed them both, but there wasn't enough proof to build a case on. As the story goes, my grandfather's paranoia began to overwhelm him. Fearing for his life, he left my mother with his brother and his wife, and just disappeared—taking his two sons with him. This was all revealed to my mother in a letter which he'd written to her before his death years later. He'd made both his sons vow not to contact my mom (their sister) until he passed away.

One afternoon I watched my mother open the mail box and begin to read the letter as she walked back up to the house.

She didn't make it—she collapsed in the front yard. I ran to try and find out what was wrong. I learned this story sitting there with her as she wept for what seemed like hours, having discovered that she had two elder brothers, and that her father, whom she'd never seen or heard from, had just passed away. It was a shattering experience for our family.

All this family history business had a deeply profound impact on me personally. Both these stories forced me to question things about my life, and the lives of others. Marriage covenant, birthing and raising children, honesty, responsibility, compassion for others, respect, love and the fallen nature of humankind—sin. Trying to learn how to process all that became a pretty heavy burden to bear. As it turned out, these events were all part of God's plan to begin imparting a desire into my heart in matters of *generational connections* (see Rom. 8:28).

> "He planted a witness in Jacob, set his Word firmly in Israel, then commanded our parents to teach it to their children so the next generation would know, and all the generations to come—know the truth and tell the stories so their children can trust in God, never forget the works of God but keep his commands to the letter."
>
> ~Ps. 78:5-7 (MSG)

The last verse is not as dramatic as the first two, but for me it is much more personal since it deals directly with my father.

I grew up in a great home with godly parents. They were wonderful to me. I don't know how my life with them could have been better—blessed as I was. My dad had a solid understanding of how to be the head of our home and to provide, cover, and love his wife, and his only child—me. Nonetheless he told me something one day that relates directly to the stories you've just read.

One day when I was still a baby the pressure of a new family, livelihood issues, and, I imagine, some generalized fear took hold on him. On his way to work one morning he decided to just drive away and never look back. Keep in mind that he knew the first story about his grandfather, the kidnapping, and the abuse. But he didn't know anything about the other story involving my mom's childhood and the situation with her father. That all came out years later, as I said. As it turned out, the Holy Ghost got my dad's attention that morning in the car, and before he got too many miles away, he made a decision to face life as it had been given him. So he turned around, drove back to Nashville, and went to work. He lived that way for another 40 years or so. In the year I turned 40, he turned 68 and went home to be in the eternal Presence of God.

After my father passed away these three stories all came together as a song. The inspiration for it came from a book I was reading by Gordan Dalby entitled, *Fathers & Sons*. In it Dalby commented on something he'd discovered in his ministry to men across the country. He always asked in his seminars for the men who were present to stand up and state the names of the men who had proceeded them generationally in their families. During his years of ministry he discovered just how quickly our culture was losing touch with its roots. Few men could go back past two generations before them. That all prompted me to write the song and it prompts me even today to say this:

PARTICULAR PONDERING(S)

I am Richard Wayne Berry; the son of William Lee Berry; the son of Rufus Henry Berry; the son of John Lee Berry... who was driven away from his family for acts of an ungodly nature.

My father broke the cycle of iniquity when he turned his car around that morning so many years ago. After several years of personal struggle and running away in my own life, I came to terms with how I should try to live before my Lord. By God's grace and under His mercy I am still standing my ground for the sake of His kingdom. Now my son, Jesse Aaron Berry has the chance to add his story to mine and our forefathers.

I've shared this song lyric and these background stories with you in order to make the following observation. The Biblical meaning of the word *salvation* is much broader than the receiving of forgiveness for our sins and being assured of our promised rewards in heaven when we die. In Scripture, salvation has as much to do with deliverance in this world as it does our hope in the afterlife. The word *deliverance* carries the meaning of... *Aid; Victory; Health (physically or spiritually); Welfare; Liberty; and Rescue (physically or morally).*

The salvation (deliverance) of the Lord has been at work in my life since before I was born (Ps. 139:13-16). It has worked a cleansing purification in my temporal bloodline by transfusing it with the pure and holy, sacrificial, atoning blood of the Lamb, Christ Jesus, my Lord, and Savior. Not only has my family history been cleaned up, my life in the present—the now—is still being purified daily. And my eternal future has already been perfected—before the days of my destiny have even come to be (Ps. 31:14-16).

This is all a mystery. It is also a divine gift from my heavenly Father (Ja. 1:17). And that gives me all the reason I need to testify to His goodness here "in the land of the living" (Ps. 116:5-9).

This testimony is a declaration of His deliverance from a *generation curse*. Blessed be the name of the Lord!

Posted by WORSHIP ARTS at 7:30 AM

Wednesday, July 1, 2009
REPENTANT WORSHIP
(Case Studies)

I'm gonna cut right to the chase. It appears to me that brokenness and contrition are in danger of becoming obsolete practices within the fellowship of the saints. The contemporary church seems to have lost much of its understanding of what it means to repent of sin, turn away from unrighteousness, and pursue an upright relationship with the Lord in holy reverence. There, I've said it.

> *"The fear of (reverence for) the Lord is the beginning of wisdom."*
>
> ~Pro. 1:7, addition mine

I have no intension of trying to build a case for my reasoning that will convince you that my observation is correct. There's really little point in such an endeavor. A better course of action, kingdom-wise, would be to let God's Word do the convincing—and convicting.

What follows are three brief case studies from scriptural accounts of what repentance looks like. They serve as an outline for a teaching series of mine focused on repentant worship. Perhaps they will give you some incentive for your own self-study. That way you may be better able to see what the Holy Ghost reveals to you in regards to living a lifestyle of repentance (see Rom. 12:1 MSG).

I'll begin with a couple of working definitions.

Repentance: To be sorry / To turn back or away from / To return to the starting point / To retreat or backtrack. To think differently / To change or transform / To refashion (metamorphose).

Contrition: To collapse (physically or mentally). From words meaning to crush, crumble or break (into pieces).

Case Study #1: Ps. 51

David: Personal moral failures resulted in David's acts of repentant worship.
- Confrontation (being uncovered)
- Confession (verbal acknowledgement of sin)
- Conversion (actions that back up the words of confession)

v.1 David's plea for grace and forgiveness is based on God's nature (i.e. His lovingkindness and compassion).

v.2 David is specific regarding his failures, acknowledging three areas of accountability:
- Transgressions (violation of moral or ethical law)
- Iniquity (habitual sin patterns—often with a generational base)
- Sin (missing the mark or falling short of God's righteous standards)

v.3 David owns his stuff. He blames no one but himself.

v.4 David sees all the violations as being first and foremost between himself and God. With that being the case, he throws himself on God's merciful justice.

vs.5-9 He begins with a verbal confession.

vs.10-12 His confession flows freely and deeply (open and honest).

vs.13-14 He speaks forth the end desire of his pleading before the Father (righteous restoration).

vs.15-17 He shows that he has a deep understanding and intimate knowledge of who God is and what He can do (faith in action).

Vs.18-19 David sees a clear connection between how he walks with God and its effect on the fellowship of the saints as well. He has a corporate heart concerned with favor and restoration for himself and others.

Corporate Heart: David considers how his own sin can/is having a direct effect on his personal witness (testimony) and also on the lives of those he could/should be able to minister to. Such a perspective as this is becoming rare indeed within the body of Christ.

The key to unlocking restoration and renewal in David's life is his offering of confession. This is a model of how a personal witness and ministry can be purified through acts of repentant worship.

LAMENT

A broken and a contrite heart
O God, You will not despise
Against You only I have sinned
I have fallen once again
I come to You in emptiness

Fill me with Your holiness
Create in me a heart that's clean
Draw me to Your side and then
Restore me with Your steadfast love

Have mercy on my wickedness
O God, I seek Your graciousness
Wash away iniquity
Remove transgression far from me
I come to You in brokenness
Fill with Your righteousness
(W. Berry / See & Say Songs, BMI)

Case Study #2: Daniel 9

Daniel: The act of identificational repentance positioned Daniel "in the gap" for the nation of Israel and himself (Ezek. 22:30). His worshipful prayers became a force "on earth as is in heaven" to set the stage for breakthrough and deliverance.

Every act of worship is an act of warfare.

Vs.1 and 2 Show Daniel to be a man of study and meditation (a theologian)
v.3 He pays a price to connect with his burden
- Prayer (mystical connection)
- Supplication (verbal utterance)
- Fasting (physical expenditure)
- Sackcloth and Ashes (outward signs of inward brokenness)

vs.4-19 Daniel takes up his repentant worship for all Israel and pours himself unreservedly into it. He reminds the Lord of His "compassion and forgiveness" (v.9) and states that the Lord should hear and respond "for Thine own sake" (v.19). He's more concerned about God's name and reputation than he is his own or that of the people.

vs.20-23 Show that the moment Daniel stepped over into such repentant worship was when God began releasing His captive people (v.23).

This is a model of how someone's acts of repentant worship can serve as a means for others to be released and restored to freedom.

Case Study #3: Jonah 1, 2

Jonah: Disobedience to God's call and direction give us the context for how and why repentant worship took place in Jonah's life.

vs.1, 2 God's word comes to Jonah with direction for him to carry out, "arise and go to Nineveh." Jehovah wants to release a call for repentance and restoration to the residents of a city whose "wickedness has come up" before the Lord (NASB). And, he wants the call for repentance to come forth from a servant entrusted to carry the will of God's word forth to the people. Jonah has the opportunity and good fortune to be chosen of the Lord for this task.

v.3 Jonah's response is to disregard his calling and try to run away from it. By doing so he has placed himself in the position of moving out of God's will which will in turn bring him to a point where his own wickedness rises up before the Lord. The effect of that will mean that Jonah will find himself in need of repentance as a result of his own spiritual insubordination.

v.4 The storm that the Lord releases is Jonah's wake up call meant to (re)awaken him to the reality of what it means to disobey the voice of the Spirit. Note that the storm is not a punishment—it is an attention getter. This insight can serve as a good perspective for how to look at tough or awkward circumstances in our own lives if/when they come. Trying to rebuke the devil is not always the best choice to make. Sometimes the "storm" that's hitting us is in fact God's way of getting our attention.

Selah…pause and consider.

vs.5-16 You can read the story for yourself. Most of us probably know it well. It sets the stage for Jonah to come to terms with his need for personal repentant worship.

v.17 Note that the "great fish" is not God's wrathful vengeance on Jonah for his failure to obey God's direction. It is in fact God's means of providing deliverance from drowning. Yes, really.

Chapter 2 provides us with a vivid picture of what it means to be broken and contrite before the Lord in confession and repentance.

From within the belly of the fish Jonah begins to worship in a way most profound. He understands very well that he has been delivered from drowning by being swallowed up. What *could* be viewed as going from bad to worse (from being thrown overboard to being swallowed) isn't how Jonah responds to the situation at all. Rather, he begins to see his current circumstances (in the fish's belly) as a place of sanctuary. It becomes *a holy place* of worship.

Vs.2-6 Jonah prays a most beautiful prayer of thanksgiving

seemingly trapped within a place with no way out. Even though his predicament could seem hopeless, he nonetheless sees his surroundings as being provision from the Lord as a means of escape from the sea which would have surely taken his life. He purposes to pursue the Presence. The last line of verse 6 clearly shows us that something major has happened to Jonah. He has experienced a Divine Encounter! The text says, "but Thou hast brought up my life from the pit (the sea), O Lord my God." (NASB)." How powerful!

v.7-9 Gives us the specific text of Jonah's prayers of worship and repentance. His faith and trust has risen up before the Lord "into Thy holy temple" (v.7). He offers his thanksgiving and renews his vow (of obedience) to His Sovereign. Then He acknowledges that his salvation (deliverance) has come from Jehovah.

Note that his prayer is released from within the place of his apparent captivity (the fish's belly). His seeming entrapment has been converted into a sanctuary, and his praises unto the Lord arises *before his deliverance* (see Isa. 54:1 / Rom. 8:28 / Phil. 4:4-8).

This is a model of how God's plan and purpose can be fulfilled through someone's acts of repentant worship for moving in disobedience to a call upon their life.

To refocus, please refer to the working definitions for repentance and for contrition.

It's clear to see that Jonah's story provides us with a testimony of how both those precepts have done their work in a deep and profound way. But, that's not the end of this story. There are two more chapters to consider.

I'd be doing an injustice to the Word by leaving the rest of the drama out. A comprehensive examination of Jonah's comings and goings requires that the ending be at least mentioned. Please read chapters 3–4.

Jonah did in fact repent, and he went on to be the agent of change that God had appointed him to be. By doing so, the entire population of Nineveh received salvation through Jehovah's righteous acts of lovingkindness (Jon. 3:6-10). However, a turn of events took place thereafter which makes the point of the story even more important to our own lives and times.

After such a glorious and dynamic set of events had taken place (revival) Jonah begins to *flesh out* by becoming quite the malcontent. His grumbling and complaining before the Lord are truly a sad testimony to how our own walk in the Spirit can often become misguided. By becoming so carnal and self-centered after the outpouring of the Holy Ghost over the entire city, Jonah exhibits traits of human fallenness which we all still struggle with to this day.

We are called as servants unto our Lord, Christ Jesus. It is our duty (our responsibility) to listen to and obey the Spirit's leading in all matters.

In order to maintain the vitality and power of the Presence in our lives, God has established the process of restoration for us in our fallen-temporal-condition.

This process is laid out clearly for us in 1 Jn. 1:6-10 in order to teach us that conviction leads us to confession, and then repentance in order that we may be restored, renewed, and re-established in our witness and ministry.

Selah…pause and consider.

Posted by WORSHIP ARTS at 5:32 AM

Saturday, August 1, 2009
THE NOT-SO-CONSTANT GARDENER

I live in a neighborhood where several of the houses have fairly large yards. Those that surround us at the "Berry-Patch" have at least an acre or so. Our property is just a little shy of two. I do a lot of reading, praying, studying, and all-round-pondering (i.e. worship) sitting on our patio in the backyard—weather permitting.

Today (7/6/09) as I was sitting there, the Holy Ghost began to speak to me about kingdom stuff using the garden in the yard that's directly behind our house. This is what took place:

In late spring the gentleman that lives there drove a pickup truck into his side yard filled with some type of specially prepared fertilizer. It came in rolls, and there were several. He unloaded them and then began to break them apart with a shovel, a hoe, and his bare hands. No other preparation had taken place, but I assumed that he had plans to plant something there.

One morning some two weeks later, another truck showed up in his driveway. This time it had one of those small backhoes on a small trailer behind it. The man driving the truck unloaded the Bobcat, and in no time at all he had plowed out a good-sized plot of ground that was clearly intended to become a produce garden.

A day or two later my neighbor was out there for several hours doing some very exacting work. He measured off the plowed plot; then measured off evenly laid out and divided rows within it; then he took heavy twine and stretched it out across the entire space. I was very impressed—I could see he had a purpose for this space having invested his time, money, and energy on it.

Then not many days later I saw him out again. This time he had what appeared to be some type of special wooden box in his hands. I watched him kneel down and begin to carefully take several packages of seed out of it. And again he spent the better part of a day patiently planting those things that he clearly intended to nurture in hopes of reaping a harvest of the fruits (and vegetables) of his labor. At least that was his apparent intention.

Instead, something else happened. Either he got distracted by other things; or his work schedule forced him to readjust his priorities; or he got bored with the project; or he just got too lazy to bother with it. I don't know for certain why things changed. But they clearly did. I saw him out there only one more time early one evening. He set up a sprinkler and began to water what he'd so carefully planted. Since that evening, there's been no more attention given to the ground or the seeds in it.

Today (some 2 ½ months later) as I look out across my yard and over into his, this is what I saw: Weeds!

If you were to look at his garden spot today having not noticed the work that he did several weeks ago, you'd be hard pressed to even know that the area was any different from the rest of his yard. Now it just looks like a section that needs a good mowing. There's nothing there except for the weeds, due to lack of attention. No, that's not totally true. The twine is still stretched out across what was once plowed ground. If you walked over near it you'd still be able to see that it divides up the land into rows meant for something besides weeds. There is one stalk of corn about 10 inches high and what appears to be a plant that wanted to be squash. But, a garden it isn't—not even close.

As I surveyed the scene, the Holy Ghost spoke to me regarding our lives in the Spirit. This is what I heard Him say:

Planning, preparation, and intention are all necessary things in order to set aside a space in our lives for the seed of God's Word to be planted. That's called consecration. However, once the seed is sown it will require something more from us. That's call self-discipline. Ongoing, regular and diligent attention will have to be factored into our schedules (our lifestyles) if we hope to have anything coming up from the seed that can be used to feed our hungry souls. Without care and proper attention, kingdom seeds are choked out by temporal weeds (see Mark 4:19).

> *"In simple humility, let our gardener, God, landscape you with the Word, making a salvation-garden of your life."*
>
> ~Ja. 1:21 (MSG)

VEGETABLES

I'm gonna be round my vegetables
I'm gonna chow down my vegetables
I love you most of all
My favorite vege-table

THE NOT-SO-CONSTANT GARDENER

If you brought a big brown bag of them home
I'd jump up and down and hope you'd toss me a carrot

I'm gonna keep well my vegetables
Cart off and sell my vegetables
I love you most of all
My favorite vege-table

I tried to kick the ball but my tenny flew right off
I'm red as a beet 'cause I'm so embarassed

I know that you'll feel better
When you send us in
Your letter an'
Tell us the name of your
Your favorite vege-table

(Brian Wilson / Van Dyke Parks
Lyrics © Universal Music Publishing Group B. Used by permission)

Posted by WORSHIP ARTS at 10:00 AM

Tuesday, September 1, 2009
A GOOD GIFT
(Mt. 7:7-11)

"God, high above, sees far below; no matter the distance, He knows everything about us."

~Ps. 138:6 (MSG)

I've recently returned from my 10th sojourn to the continent of Africa. The mystery and majesty of what God has deposited in that land and those who dwell there always amazes and humbles me. The kindness and hospitality of the African people is often overwhelming. And the grandeur of the Creator's handiwork revealed through nature truly is astounding to witness first hand (Rom. 1:20). But on this trip my Lord's involvement in the smallest details of my life has prompted me to give testimony to His Fatherly benevolence to His children.

Here's what happened:

I've wanted an instrument from Africa for several years. It's called a Mbira. History traces its roots to the nation of Zimbabwe hundreds of years ago.

You might know of it as a *thumb piano*, but that's not a term Africans care for. That's a name coined by the English, and I feel that it is a slight to the region and the indigenous craftsmen who designed and perfected how it is to be played.

Pardon my multi-cultural venting. Now, getting back to my testimony…

Through prayerful contacts I have with some brethren in Zimbabwe I managed to purchase one made locally. I was overjoyed to finally get my hands on one I could call my own. Having researched its use I knew that playing it correctly—the Shona way—takes patience, practice, prayer, and perseverance from anyone interested enough and serious enough to begin the process of learning. I also knew that the first real problem I might encounter would be related to how it is tuned and kept in tune after the long trip back to the U.S. and the months and years of hands-on-attention it would take to eventually coax music out of it. So, connecting with someone in America that could perhaps assist me was a priority once I returned home.

As a worship pastor, minstrel, and psalmist unto the Lord I take the spiritual act of consecration very seriously (see Josh. 3:5 / 1 Chron. 15:11, 12 / 2 Chron. 29:5). So, in one of the services I was to minister the Word, I made a request of those attending the gathering and of one of the bishops who was also there to bring a word from the Lord. I asked him and the congregation to allow me a few moments at the beginning of the service in order for him to anoint my Mbira and me with oil and to pray a prayer of consecration for kingdom service. They all graciously consented to do so. Having done that, I'm taking to heart what we did and I'm trusting the Holy Ghost to honor my request for my musicianship and my instrument to be used in any way that will glorify Christ Jesus, and advance the kingdom here on earth.

This is where the really amazing part comes into play: I've

been home only two weeks. Nonetheless the Lord has already made a way for me to link up with the best known female Mbira player in America. It turns out, through Divine happenstance, that she will be conducting a weekend workshop in October, in Chicago—where our daughter just happens to live.

My wife and I are headed there for a visit in three weeks. Arrangements were firmed up today for me to take my Mbira with me and leave it with my daughter. She is going to drop it off at the workshop—which just happens to be only 1 ½ miles from her apartment (in a city of 2.8 million). The Mbira master has agreed to set mine up properly making certain that it's tuned according to the Zimbabwe (Shona) tradition.

I've said all that to say this: The little things (the very little things) that are important to us are also important to our heavenly Father.

Someone who's reading this perhaps needed to be reminded of that.

YOU ARE LORD (Kenya Song) (Ps. 138:4-6)

Over every tribe and nation, over every generation
Over all of Your creation, You are Lord
You are awesome, high and holy, but You bring comfort to the lowly
Thru Your presence and Your glory, You are Lord

Over wilderness and wasteland, and in every place where we stand
All of life is held in Your hand, You are Lord
Over every joy and sorrow, over Mount Kilimanjaro
Yesterday, today, tomorrow, You are Lord

A GOOD GIFT

Over every hopeless pilgrim, over all who seek Your kingdom
May Your prefect will be done, for You are Lord
Till the day of Your appearing, as eternity is nearing
I'll tell all within my hearing, You are Lord

CHORUS:
I worship You, I worship You, Lord
I worship You, I worship You, Lord

By: W. Berry / See & Say Songs, BMI

Posted by WORSHIP ARTS at 1:45 PM

Thursday, October 1, 2009
MORNING HAS BROKEN
(Prayers of Thanksgiving)

There are several things that I try to be faithful in as I offer daily prayers. I'd like to say that most of the items on my prayer list get covered each day—but that's not always the case. However, there are two expressions of thanksgiving that I start my day off with pretty much without fail. I thank the Lord for *bird song* and *worship on the wind*.

The *bird song* prayer was birthed sitting on my patio in the backyard of the Berry-Patch one morning just before dawn. In the spring, summer and early fall I tend to try and get outside as early as possible. I'm often outside and find myself in the space where darkness is just beginning to turn into light. When that happens, three things stir in my spirit reminding me that:

- God's daily mercy shows up "new every morning"
- I'm witnessing the birth of a new day
- The night silence is being broken by the sound of birds offering up songs of praise

The other prayer point—*worship on the wind*—is something I've already addressed in a previous blog entitled "Wind Blown Worship." If you've read it then you understand what I mean when I use that phrase. If you haven't read it, you can backtrack through my other postings. Then maybe you'll start to hear things in the breeze yourself.

MERCY COMES CALLING

While it's still dark outside, a supernatural thing's occurring
Light begins to rise, and life starts to stirring
Then suddenly without warning, another day is dawning

As mercy comes calling, mercy comes calling
Mercy comes calling, it's new every morning

Night silence fills the air, as the atmosphere is changing
For those with ears to hear, creation wakes up singing
God's Sovereign hand is forming, a reason for rejoicing

As mercy comes calling...

When the sun runs out its course, the shadows start descending
An indescribable force, brings another day to an ending
As I lay down for sleeping, I yield my soul to His keeping

As mercy comes calling...

By: W. Berry / See & Say Songs, BMI

Posted by WORSHIP ARTS at 12:04 PM

Sunday, November 1, 2009
ENTERING IN

I want to unpack that term "entering in" with you in order to consider exactly what it means. The way it is most often used in congregations is something like let's all "enter into God's Presence," or perhaps, "it's time to enter into worship." There are several ways of expressing the concept—I'm sure you know the varied phrases. I'm not too interested in the specific language that you might use, however. What I'm really wanting to get at is the meaning behind the term itself.

As a worship pastor for the last 13 years, and a worship leader for some 15 years prior to that, I've come to believe that many (most) worshipers don't really have a clear understanding of what it means when we say we're "entering in" as we're gathered to enthrone God upon our praises (Ps. 22:3).

There's a lot I'd like to say, but I am purposed to be as concise as possible with my comments. To do so I'm going to borrow an example from a message I recently heard given by Bishop Joseph Garlington. It's one of the best explanations I've ever heard dealing with this topic. And, since I am in relationship with Bishop, I know he won't mind if I use it—especially having given him credit for his insights.

Here's a paraphrased version of what he said:

When we turn on our T.V.s or radios (lap tops and iPhones) to listen to a program that we are interested in, the people involved (cast and crew) aren't sitting in a studio somewhere waiting for us to tune in before they begin. Of course not. They begin their program with or without us. At the moment we link up with what's already *in progress* we are *entering in* to what was taking place before we ever turned the power on. Our involvement—at whatever level we choose—begins when we engage in what's already happening. In other words, the program—or church service—can, will, and does take place with or without us. But, in order for us to share in the experience, we have to engage with those who are already actively taking part in the presentation.

I think Bishop's comments are spot on. The process is the same in matters of corporate praise and worship. Saints and angels on earth and in heaven above are pro-active in praise and worship all the time (24/7/365). It's non-stop, with no breaks and no pauses. Praise and worship is ongoing, constant, and eternal. So, when we're *entering in* to the adoration and exaltation of the Lord, our God, the offerings aren't beginning with us. We're not starting anything—we're joining a program already in progress.

Selah…pause and consider.

I suppose some Scriptural support would be in order here to ground what I'm saying. So, consider this please:

"For you have not come to a mountain that can be touched and to a blazing fire, and to darkness and gloom and

whirlwind, and to the blast of a trumpet and the sound of words which sound was such that those who heard begged that no further word be spoken to them... you have come to Mount Zion and to the city of the living God, the heavenly Jerusalem, and to myriads of angels, to the general assembly and church of the firstborn who are enrolled in heaven, and to God, the Judge of all, and to the spirits of the righteous made perfect, and to Jesus, the mediator of a new covenant, and to the sprinkled blood, which speaks better than the blood of Abel."

~Heb. 12:18, 19, 22-24

Note please in verse 22 where it says that we "have come to Mount Zion." The word *come* in its base language is in the active tense, meaning that it has already taken place. The passage is leading us to understand that we have (in terms of eternity) already "entered in" to the scene the text goes on to describe in grand and glorious details. Saints, we're in already! Therefore all that's required of us is to act like we know that and respond accordingly.

BOW DOWN

Bow down before the Lord
Worship Him, Oh worship Him
Bow down before our God
Enter in, Oh enter in

Consuming fire, sweet perfume
His awesome presence fills this room
This is holy ground, so come and bow down

ENTERING IN

Holy, Holy, Holy Lord of hosts
Saints and angels give Him glory
In the Holy Ghost
(David Baroni and Tony Sutherland
Integrity's Hosanna Music, Used by permission)

Posted by WORSHIP ARTS at 9:00 AM

Tuesday, December 1, 2009
THE ULTIMATE WORSHIP WARRIOR

Scripture reveals to us that Jesus is the "author and finisher" of our faith (Heb. 12:2). I take that to mean that the embodiment of a life of faithful service to God is exemplified through Christ's obedience to His Father's Sovereign will. Quite literally, our Lord modeled what it means to be a "living sacrifice" by going to the Cross as the act of redemption for all of humankind. Having had the power—and the right—to call down all the forces of heaven on His behalf (Mt. 26:53) in order to side-step Golgotha, He instead chose to yield Himself up in submission to the orders He'd received from headquarters.

His yielding (Phil. 2:7, 8) came at the zenith of the most terrifying moment of the most horrific battle that's ever taken place on earth. The warfare that raged there on skull hill that dark day was like no other confrontation that had ever taken place.

All the vile forces of hell were directly arrayed against the very throne of God in heaven. But at that juncture when divine force, supernatural power, Sovereign authority, and Holy self-determination would have seemed the only fitting way to engage in battle, an entirely unexpected strategy was implement. Rather than confront the enemy with a display of Divinity, Jesus humbled Himself on the cross (Heb. 2:9, 10, 14) and gave Himself as an act of worship.

His body raised up bruised, beaten and bloody became the glorious standard lifted up to draw all men to Him (Jn. 12:32). No weapon was used, except His own body. No fisted hand was raised in anger. Instead, His empty and opened hands were extended in complete *consecration and nailed to a cross beam. From that position He could render no blows against His adversary. The only wounds inflicted that day were the ones He took upon Himself (Isa. 53:5).

The resistance toward Satan that the Lord showed us was manifested through His act of surrender to the Father. In the middle of the warfare, worship alone became Christ's weapon of choice. Jesus trusted that His Commander-In-Chief would provide both vindication and victory as He saw fit. The resurrection accomplished both.

CONSECRATION is the setting aside of any person, place, or thing for acts of holy service. It also can mean to come with an open hand (as opposed to a closed or fisted one).

In those despairingly desperate moments on Calvary our Savior showed each of us how the life of a warrior and a worshiper could be linked together in a way most profound. There is no better way of explaining that every act of worship is an act of war than to let Scripture speak for itself:

PARTICULAR PONDERING(S)

"He stripped all the spiritual tyrants in the universe of their sham authority at the Cross and marched them naked through the streets."

~Col. 2:15 (MSG)

Posted by WORSHIP ARTS at 2:00 AM

Friday, January 1, 2010
GENERATIONAL NETWORKING

At 63 I'm considered an *old guy* in some circles. Especially in this country where I'm standing at the front of the *boomer* line. However, in other nations, and at other times in our cultural de-evolution I'd be considered—and revered—as an elder; worthy of respect and honor simply because I had earned those perks through the process of aging. Seeing things from my perspective as an *aged one*, I am concerned and saddened by what's being lost to the generations coming along behind me.

We are all suffering from the disconnections which are taking place between the young and older in matters related to living on this planet. I recently read a comment somewhere online that said we were becoming a nation of hermits slouched over our computer screens with our *BlackBerrys* in hand. That's certainly not the way our Creator intends for us to live our lives.

Scripture gives us a very clear picture of how we are to be joined together:

"And even when I am old and gray, O God, do not forsake me,

PARTICULAR PONDERING(S)

until I declare Your strength to this generation, Your power to all who are to come."

~Ps. 71:18

"For He established a testimony in Jacob and appointed a law in Israel, which He commanded our fathers that they should teach them to their children, that the generation to come might know, even the children yet to be born, that they may arise and tell them to their children, that they should put their confidence in God and not forget the works of God, but keep His commandments..."

~Ps. 78:5-7

"You were all called to travel on the same road and in the same direction, so stay together, both outwardly and inwardly. You have one Master, one faith, one baptism, one God and Father of all, who rules over all, works through all, and is present in all. Everything you are and think and do is permeated with Oneness."

~Eph. 4:4-6 (MSG)

The Biblical directive those verses call us to as believers is certainly not how we're functioning currently. Maybe somethings will occur in the future that will begin to re-establish the pattern that God's Word gives us for helping one another to grow and mature. I hope and pray that will be the case. To that end, perhaps the following observations may help to move things in that direction.

In the October edition of *AARP Magazine* (yes, really), there was an article in the Life Lessons section entitled "The Pressure To Be Wise." It referenced a video series called *Wisdom Keepers*.

In it there are a number of short interviews with older people of accomplishment—from dancers to environmentalists to writers—intended "as a motivational tool for an audience of teenagers (now known *as young adults*)." There were a couple of phrases that prompted me to post this blog up:

At 20 You Know Everything; At 70 You're Not So Sure.

One of the reasons to keep wisdom, it seems, is so you can pass it on.

There was one section in particular that addressed this topic in a very concise fashion. Margaret Atwood, a Canadian author and poet, drew on an example from the Inuit tribe from the Arctic. Regarding the process of joining the generations among the Inuit tribe, she made the following observations:

"You can't become an Elder just by getting old; it's a title bestowed by others. You never push your advice, but you offer it if asked. You can tell who the Elders are just by watching a group. They are the ones to whom the others are always bringing cups of tea. When an Elder speaks, people listen. But, they don't speak often.

"An Elder knows what to do in times of difficulty. They acquired that knowledge by having endured hard times before. As one of their old sayings puts it, 'Good judgment comes from experience; experience comes from bad judgment.'"

She goes on to make these comments based on her cultural studies from history:

"In earlier societies, especially those living in harsh environments, at a time when the life expectancy was 35 or so, the rare individual living to 60 would have seen many more times of crisis than the younger people. He or she would have had a better idea of how to face those dangers. In traditional Japan it was the custom to tear down and rebuild wooden temples at set intervals, so that the rebuilt temple would exactly resemble its predecessor. Three generations of master craftsmen were always employed: the apprentices, who were learning; the master craftsmen of middle years, who had already lived through one temple rebuilding; and the oldest generation, who'd been through the process twice before and could coach the other two."

So, here's something for all of you apprentices and middle year folks to consider—from one of your elders. Instead of setting all us Baby Boomers adrift in tiny little boats with limited rations when we reach our 65th birthday, perhaps you could consider making space in your hearts for the principles of Scripture I mentioned above to work some kingdom renewal among us.

I'm just thinking out loud. At least I think I am. It's past my bedtime isn't it?

Posted by WORSHIP ARTS at 10:04 AM

Monday, February 1, 2010
SALVATION & SANCTIFICATION

"Work out your own salvation with fear and trembling."
~Phil. 2:12

God gives us our salvation in and through Christ Jesus, our Lord and Savior. Once we've received it, our responsibility is to develop it to maturity through yielded and obedient submission to the Holy Ghost.

Salvation is simple.
Sanctification isn't.

Salvation takes a moment.
Sanctification takes a lifetime.

Salvation requires yielding to the Holy Ghost once.
Sanctification requires yielding again, and again, and again…

Salvation is a giving up of our lives.
Sanctification is a giving up of our rights.

PARTICULAR PONDERING(S)

Salvation costs us nothing (Christ Jesus paid for it with His life).
Sanctification costs us a great deal (we pay for it with our life).

Salvation saves individuals.
Sanctification purifies and perfects those who have been redeemed.

Salvation unlocks the doorway into God's kingdom,
Sanctification carries us further—and deeper—into God's kingdom.

"To go through the door is not necessarily to live in the house."
　　　　　　　　　　Knowing Christ Today by Dallas Willard

Posted by WORSHIP ARTS at 7:22 AM

Monday, March 1, 2010
THE MINISTRY OF OBSCURITY

"Think of yourselves the way Christ Jesus thought of himself. He had equal status with God but didn't think so much of himself that he had to cling to the advantages of that status no matter what. Not at all. When the time came, he set aside the privileges of deity and took on the status of a slave, became human! Having become human, he stayed human. It was an incredibly humbling process. He didn't claim special privileges. Instead, he lived a selfless, obedient life and then died a selfless, obedient death—and the worst kind of death at that—a crucifixion."

~Phil. 2:5-8 (MSG)

The KJV says that Jesus "made himself of no reputation." Scripture instructs us to follow the example of Christ in this matter of drawing attention to ourselves, our rights, privileges, self-serving goals and personal aspirations. So, how come we don't do that? Seems to me that's a fair question to pose considering how totally different most of us approach our lives.

PARTICULAR PONDERING(S)

The call that our culture and the world system in general places before us is to climb the ladder of success all the way to the top if we can. We're taught that by our well-meaning parents for the most part. That gets reinforced by our educational system, the social sciences, the entertainment business, and our media-driven culture. In fact, most every aspect of our interpersonal relationships seem to work more to our liking when we are the ones being pleased by how others treat us. I wonder what's become of the Golden Rule? (see Luke 6:31).

I've been trying to come to terms with a passage from Scripture for the last couple of years. It continues to be a real struggle for me to reconcile my lifestyle to what it says. Ponder this: when we read Heb. 11 we find a long list of saints who are presented to us as role models for their actions of extreme faith. However, toward the end of the chapter, included in that listing there is a nameless grouping. As unidentified to us as they are, the writer of Hebrews goes so far as to elevate their status to a high and exalted level when he states in verse 38 that "the world was not worthy" of such people. Then he goes on to say that they all died "having not received the promise" of what they were living for.

Many today would say that these *faith heroes* were failures due to not getting what they were after while they were alive here on earth. It would appear that they missed their entitlements. However, that's not what the Bible says. That's not what I would say either.

And you—what would you say?

Posted by WORSHIP ARTS at 8:00 AM

Thursday, April 1, 2010
WHY WORSHIP

Some 15+ years ago I came across a wonderful song written by Lynn DeShazo titled "Be Magnified." The opening line drove me to my knees.

"I have made You too small in my eyes, oh Lord, forgive me."

That phrase linked up in my memory with a book I'd read several years prior to hearing Lynn's song. It was titled *Your God Is Too Small,* by J. B. Phillips. Such a concept is humbling to consider.

The idea of viewing God from a narrowed and shallow perspective can create a seemingly insurmountable problem for saints, both individually as well as corporately. Such a limited vista of God and His kingdom has stifled believers and derailed numbers of fellowships over the years.

There are several things that can cause one's perspective to turn inwardly myopic. Addressing them would take far more time and consideration than is appropriate in a format such as this one. So, for now, I'll only comment on one in particular which tends to try and squeeze God into our little boxes of belief. In specific I'm addressing our worship theology, or lack thereof—the study of why we believe as we do about matters related to the Father, Son, and Holy Ghost. The stuff of God's kingdom. Know what I mean?

"Without a solid foundational theology, worship becomes an exercise in self-expression."
Enthroned On Our Praise, by T. Pierce

Here's what I see taking place within our churches in the U.S. and throughout the nations-at-large. In the process of going contemporary we've learned the *how* and *what* of worship well, but we've discarded much of the *why*. In other words, we've figured out how worship should manifest in our congregations, and we know what to do to make that happen. But we no longer give much thought to why we worship.

In essence we've allowed our "too small" view of God to restrict our ability to reach out beyond ourselves and our limited and temporal understanding of Him. In doing so, we are, in a sense, restraining the Lord's ability to increase within us.

The end result of such a process is that much of the mystery of the kingdom and the world of wonders that life in the Spirit affords us has been diminished.

We need a bigger God than the one we currently worship. So, for the sake of enlargement consider the following passages from Scripture:

"He spreads the skies over unformed space,
hangs the earth out in empty space.
He pours water into cumulus cloud-bags
and the bags don't burst.

He makes the moon wax and wane,
putting it through its phases.
He draws the horizon out over the ocean,
sets a boundary between light and darkness.
The thunder crashes and rumbles in the skies.
Listen! It's God raising his voice!
By his power he stills sea storms,
by his wisdom he tames sea monsters.
With one breath he clears the sky,
with one finger he crushes the sea serpent.
And this is only the beginning, a mere whisper of his rule."
~Job 26:5-14 (MSG)

Selah…pause and consider.

Posted by WORSHIP ARTS at 6:00 AM

Thursday, April 9, 2009
GOD'S GOT YOU COVERED

"You are my hiding place; You preserve me from trouble; You surround me with songs of deliverance."

~Ps. 32:7

Selah…pause and consider.

I do a lot of pondering. I turn things over in my head, heart, and spirit. I examine, re-consider, and generally think about stuff in ways that some folks don't want to be bothered by. So be it. We're all "fearfully and wonderfully made" ya know (Ps. 139:14).

There's a word (besides *nuts*) for someone who filters life that way.

Contemplative: Marked by or given to contemplation.

A contemplative person practices contemplation.

Contemplation:
- Concentration on spiritual things as a form of private devotion
- Acts of considering with attention [*Midrash*: Hebrew for *study*]

- The act of regarding steadily)

Here's a portion of a recent pondering that I thought I'd blogify 4 u: The verse I've quoted above tells us that we're surrounded by "songs of deliverance." The KJV says God will "compass" us about. To compass (or encompass) something means to cover it from every possible angle and perspective—North, South, East, West—as well as above and beneath. In other words, the Spirit of God daily covers us with such deliverance songs. From every direction we turn, from where we stand, and to wherever we might ascend—songs (KJV says "shouts") of deliverance are there waiting to be heard, sung, and appropriated into our lives.

Did you know that? Can you hear them?

More about all that in the daze ahead (see Ps. 139:7-10). For now, try a little Selah-ness.

Commenting on the phrase "You shall surround me with songs of deliverance," Charles Spurgeon says this:

"What a golden sentence! David is surrounded with song and with dancing mercies, all proclaiming the triumphs of grace. There is no breach in the circle; it surrounds him. On all sides, he hears music, in front, hope sounds the cymbals, and behind, gratitude beats the timbrel. Right and left, above and beneath, the air resounds with joy."

From *The Treasury of David* by Charles Spurgeon

Posted by WORSHIP ARTS at 7:05 AM

May 1st, 2010
PONDERING PRAYER

Last month I had a kingdom encounter of sorts…
I was attending a gathering of some 350-400 folks who are active in ministry. During one of the sessions we were given several questions to respond to. There was a monitoring system in place whereby our responses could be recorded the moment we gave them. Then, in real time, they could be tallied on computer by percentage and posted up on screens in order for everyone to know how the group had answered. One of the questions caught my attention at a base level in my spirit. It had to do with what order of priority we gave to three specific things. They were:
- Prayer
- Reading God's Word
- Preparation for Public Ministry (study and research)

The response(s) in a room filled with pastoral and staff leadership was profound. As a group prayer was positioned first on our collective list by almost 70%.

I have to be transparent here with what I'm going to say next. What came up inside me was this question: If prayer is really that important to us, then I wonder how much time during the day we each spend devoted to it? I may be way off base here, but I think that if we were each approached to give our personal answer to that question most of us would admit we spend far less time in intercession and active listening to the voice of the Holy Ghost than we'd really care to acknowledge.

Following just a few days after that encounter, I read the following comments in a book by Richard Foster titled *Life With God: Reading the Bible for Spiritual Transformation*:

"The church in the West is like roses that have been cut from their bush—they still have some blossom showing but they are wilting because they have been severed from their roots." Foster went on to say, "for restoration (rebirth) to take place the root system would first need to be reestablished. Prayer is the root system. And it is a life of prayer that needs to be reestablished in our lives. What is so needed today is not individualized prayer experiences that we can turn on or off at will like a faucet, but prayer as a constantly flowing life."

He continued by sharing about how such insights were linked to experiences that he'd had while visiting with Christians in Korea. There were several components of their prayer life that he mentioned in specific. They were: Intensity; Determined Persistence; Instant Power Engagement; Longing Love; Heartfelt Sorrow; Pain and Agony. He commented that such components as those "can only be received humbly through lived experience."

I wonder what events will have to take place in our busy, distracted, and temporal lives in order for such attributes to become the building blocks which form the prayers we offer on behalf of humanity and this spiritually deprived/depraved world we're living in?

Selah…pause and consider.

PART 2
REVELANT & RANDOM

A Biblical Perspective
CORPORATE UNITY & ENTHRONING GOD

"But You are holy, You who *inhabit the **praises of Israel."
~Ps. 22:3 (NHEB)

*Some translations use the phrase "enthroned on the praises."
**The word praises is tehillah, meaning laudation—as with hymn(s). Generally speaking, it has to do with singing in unity, or if you will, united in harmony.

"...not avoiding worshiping together, as some do, but spurring each other on, especially as we see the Big Day approaching."
~See Heb. 10:19-25 (MSG)

Here's a broader perspective on the same text (Ps. 22:3): In the KJV it reads, *"But thou art holy, O thou that inhabitest the praises of Israel."* If you unpack the word *inhabitest* here's what you'll find:

In Hebrew it is yashab, *meaning to sit down (as judge); to dwell, to remain; to settle, to marry; to make to abide, to endure. To establish a habitation (to keep house). To tarry.*

PARTICULAR PONDERING(S)

There's so much meaning contained in that word which in turn relates directly to what's taking place when God is, in fact, enthroned (*yashab*) on the praises of His people. There's much more going on when that takes place than most of us think. Follow…

The text says that God is enthroned on our praises. Ever wonder what that means? Well, to me it says that our praises build a throne for God to sit on (be enthroned on / inhabit). Considered from a supernatural or super-spiritual viewpoint, the language implies that the very throne itself is formed out of the praises being offered during congregational worship. Bear in mind that the word *praises* in the verse is *tehillah* meaning corporate singing. In other words, the offering of united voices which is herein defined as multi-voiced singing, united into one congregational voice—unity of purpose, intent, and sacrifice.

Worship is obedient service manifesting through self-sacrifice.

If you're interested, I've expanded my views on Ps. 22:3 in my book, *PONDERING(S)* in the section titled, "Enthroning God," available at fine online booksellers everywhere.

Here's an example of a corporate worship song—"we" instead of "me" focused.

JUST TO WORSHIP YOU

High above the heavens, over all the earth
You O Lord, are worthy to be praised
And through the grace You've given

CORPORATE UNITY & ENTHRONING GOD

We come before Your throne
Seeking to behold Your face
CHORUS:
Abiding in the shadow of Your Spirit
Hiding in the shelter of Your name
We have come by faith, into the holy place
Just to worship You, just to worship You
We are here just to worship You

Far above all rulers, authorities, and powers
You O Lord, it's You alone who reign
And through the grace You've given
We bow before Your throne
Honoring Your holy name
REPEAT CHORUS:

(W. Berry / See & Say Songs, BMI)

When I began digging deeper into Ps. 22:3, I noticed that the word for *enthroned* was *inhabitest* (*yashabed*) which I've mentioned already. It only appears in Scripture once. That stirred my interest big time. I figured that if it was only used in one verse then it must be very important in terms of its meaning and its application/implication. So for several years I grounded my theology on that one word usage. Then sometime later in my studies I stumbled onto an entirely different perspective regarding how this enthroning business could be understood. Here it is…

"When I went out to the gate of the city, when I took my seat in the square…"

~Job 29:7

PARTICULAR PONDERING(S)

The word "seat" in the Hebrew is *moshab* meaning to be present in a session or discussion; to abide (in place and time); to populate, assemble, dwell; to inhabit a place.

When I read that, the scene being described there looped me back to the Ps. 22:3 and God's enthronement among His people said to take place during corporate praise. I began to ponder and study how the dynamic of Ps. 22:3 was inter-related to the Job 29:7 event. When I did that, this unfolded (exploded) before me:

"When I walked downtown and sat with my friends in the public square, young and old greeted me with respect; I was honored by everyone in town.

When I spoke, everyone listened; they hung on my every word. People who knew me spoke well of me; my reputation went ahead of me. I was known for helping people in trouble and standing up for those who were down on their luck. The dying blessed me, and the bereaved were cheered by my visits.

All my dealings with people were good. I was known for being fair to everyone I met. I was eyes to the blind and feet to the lame, father to the needy, and champion of abused aliens. I grabbed street thieves by the scruff of the neck and made them give back what they'd stolen. I thought, 'I'll die peacefully in my own bed, grateful for a long and full life, a life deep-rooted and well-watered, a life limber and dew-fresh, my soul suffused with glory and my body robust until the day I die.' Men and women listened when I spoke, hung expectantly on my every word. After I spoke, they'd be quiet, taking it all in. They welcomed my counsel like spring rain, drinking it all in. When I smiled at them, they could hardly believe it; their faces lit up, their troubles took wing! I was

CORPORATE UNITY & ENTHRONING GOD

their leader, establishing the mood and setting the pace by which they lived. Where I led, they followed."

I personally believe that the scene described in that passage has a direct bearing on how congregations all over the world should understand what is taking place when God sits down *enthroned* among His people. It's not that every word of Job's explanation fits perfectly with what happens during congregational praise and worship. Rather, it's about the tone of such an event. The atmosphere that's being established becomes more meaningful. Our praise starts to focus in with a pro-active-purpose. The environment transforms into a supernaturally charged space which can then be entered as a construction site where throne-building is taking place—a gathering space where we're enthroning our Sovereign provides a time and place where He can manifest and impart to anyone and everyone, anything in any way He chooses.

That is, in fact, what a Sovereign does.

"It is madness to wear ladies' straw hats and velvet hats to church; we should all be wearing crash helmets. Ushers should issue life preservers and signal flares; they should lash us to our pews."
Annie Dillard

If/When our *corporate awareness* begins to truly comprehend and embrace what's really taking place, then the impact of our Creator reigning over us during our Sunday services will have the potential to change profoundly.

There is much more taking place spiritually when we gather to lift Him up on our praises than we've realized, dear cohorts. So much more of His Divine presence is in our midst than we've ever dared to imagine. I'd suggest that you take a moment here to re-read the passage from Job in light of what I've just shared.

Now, read Ps. 139:7-12 (also 1 Cor. 3:16), and ask yourself why we continue to anticipate His presence while beckoning Him to show up in our services when Scripture clearly states that He's everywhere all the time. He is after all, Omnipresent. Rather than awaiting (beseeching) Him to join us, we'd be more in line with the Word if we'd acknowledge that He's already abiding with us both corporately and individually.

THE BEST SEAT IN THE HOUSE

Make room, make way
We've come into His house to bless Him today
Make some noise, lift up a shout
Do what you have to do to get your worship out

CHORUS:
(Our God deserves), the best seat in the house
Lord, come and take Your rightful pace
You are due the highest honor
So we're building You a throne of praise
The heavens cannot contain You
Of that there is no doubt
We welcome Your Holy Presence
(You deserve), the best seat in the house

Take a stand, make a choice
Open up the heavens with the sound of your voice
State it clear, say it plain
Do what you've got to do to declare Him as King

REPEAT CHORUS:

(W. Berry / See & Say Songs, BMI)

A Morning Meditation
UP THERE, DOWN HERE

"[If] then you have been raised with Christ, seek the things that are above, where Christ is, seated at the right hand of God. Set your minds on things that are above, not on things that are on earth. For you have died, and your life is hidden with Christ in God."

~Col. 3:1-3 (ESV)

Observations:
1. Note the conditional word *if*. It means that what follows thereafter is meant for those who are "with Christ in God." In other words, it doesn't apply to those who aren't.
2. The first directive in the text says to "seek the things that are above", which links directly—as I understand it—to the charge which Jesus personally gave regarding spiritual priorities: "Seek first the kingdom of God and His righteousness..." (Mt. 6:33)
3. The next directive is to set our minds on things above.

That is to say we, as followers of Christ, are to view life on earth from the top down, not the bottom up (See Rom.12:2). Think *"on earth as it is in heaven"* and you'll be processing the passage well.

Have a thoughtful day...

A Pondering
PAST-TENSE POSITIONING

Take note that the text below has two components which are often and easily overlooked:
1. It is written to the redeemed of the Lord exclusively (meaning it's not intended for others who aren't "in Christ"). See also Col. 3:1-3.
2. It is past tense (meaning it has already taken place in the lives of believers)

"But you are God's chosen treasure— priests who are kings, a spiritual 'nation' set apart as God's devoted ones. He called you out of darkness to experience his marvelous light, and now he claims you as his very own. He did this so that you would broadcast his glorious wonders throughout the world."
~1 Pet. 2:9 (TPT)

That being the case, why are so many so-called Christians who express faith in their salvation—in and through Christ Jesus—living as if they have to work their way into attaining what's already actively in place?

Saints, be who you already are in Jesus. In other words... act like it.

Selah...pause and consider.

A Pondering
RECONCILIATION & AMBASSADORSHIP

> "...our knowledge of men can no longer be based on their outward lives (indeed, even though we knew Christ as a man we do not know him like that any longer). For if a man is in Christ he becomes a new person altogether—the past is finished and gone, everything has become fresh and new. All this is God's doing, for he has reconciled us to himself through Jesus Christ; and he has made us agents of the reconciliation. God was in Christ personally reconciling the world to himself—not counting their sins against them—and has commissioned us with the message of reconciliation. We are now Christ's ambassadors, as though God were appealing direct to you through us. As his personal representatives we say, 'Make your peace with God.' For God caused Christ, who himself knew nothing of sin, actually to be sin for our sakes, so that in Christ we might be made good with the goodness of God."
>
> ~2 Cor. 5:18-21 (Phillips)

I personally believe that each and every follower of Christ has been charged with two key things according to the passage presented above:

RECONCILIATION & AMBASSADORSHIP

1. We have been given the ministry of reconciliation. It's our job description.
2. We are to do our work as ambassadors for Christ. That is our job title.

With that in mind, I encourage those of you who are "born again" believers to do the following things:

1. Set time aside to watch *True Justice*, now streaming on HBO.
2. Google the "Truth and Reconciliation Commission" meetings which took place in South Africa and Rwanda. Then do some reading and research regarding the process through which they took place.

NOTE: Dig a little deeper and you'll find several movies which address that subject.

A Pondering
SMALL UP YOURSELF

I'm thinkin' 'bout developing a new start-up company called VICARIOUS VITTLES. Eye envision it as a weight loss program which those interested in losing weight can join at absolutely no cost. It would be a no calorie plan with zero carbs, no sugars, and it's gluten free.

Here's how it works: Each member who joins the program simply watches other people eat. That's it. So simple. By doing so, the lbs. will quickly start to fall away.

No contract is required, and you can opt out at any time. If however you decide to continue with the plan for an extended period of time the duration may be sort lived.

As it stands presently, I think it will be a non-prophet endeavor.

FYI: Logo design is currently in development. It'll be an empty plate with some sort of catchy/cool font showing somewhere on (or near) it. A *branding* sort of thang.

A Personal Pov
FEELIN' GROOVY

S ome folks are algorhythmically challenged. Or perhaps I should say anglorhymically. They never know which beat to clap on. Just sayin'.

2/4 or not 2/4, that is the question…
　　　　　　(a variation on Willy S.'s wording)

A Pondering
COMPUTE THIS

The Kingdom of God is the recommended-factory-compatible-operating-system for the citizens of heaven: chosen generation, royal priesthood, holy nation, peculiar people—folks like that. (1 Pet. 2:9 KJV)

WARNING: The use of any other O.S. can cause considerable damage to hard drives, personal files, and memory storage. (1 Cor. 3:16 / Luke 17:21)

Said another way, the Kingdom of God is *The Context* in which each and every aspect of living a biblically-based life of faith is to be considered, processed, and applied for spiritual growth. (See Mt. 22:21 and Jn. 8:31–32).

The Beatitudes provide start-up steps for getting the equipment up and running properly (Mt. 5:1-12). The Sermon on the Mount details the protocol for developing the entire system to its maximum performance level (Mt. 5,6, and 7).

Scripturally Speaking:

"Thy kingdom come, Thy will be done, on earth as it is in heaven."

~Mt. 6:10

"For He rescued us from the domain of darkness, and transferred us to the kingdom of His beloved Son, in whom we have redemption, the forgiveness of sins."
~Col. 1:13–14

"So if you're serious about living this new resurrection life with Christ, act like it. Pursue the things over which Christ presides. Don't shuffle along, eyes to the ground, absorbed with the things right in front of you. Look up, and be alert to what is going on around Christ—that's where the action is. See things from his perspective. Your old life is dead. Your new life, which is your real life—even though invisible to spectators—is with Christ in God. He is your life. When Christ (your real life, remember) shows up again on this earth, you'll show up, too—the real you, the glorious you. Meanwhile, be content with obscurity, like Christ."
~Col. 3:1-4 (MSG)

Pondering Re-
OR RE-PONDERING

Jean (my wife of 40 years) and I have entered the "Season of Re-." Re-tirement, Re-bootment, Re-alignment, Re-distribution, Re-establishment, and Re-etc. We are being Re-trained and Re-tooled for life and ministry in ways which Re-quire us to Re-evaluate how the coming daze are to be offered up in service for the Kingdom of God. We've decided to Re-enlist as Ambassadors for Christ (job title), carrying on as ministers of reconciliation (job description). (See 2 Cor. 5:18-21).

In keeping with our Re-commitment to Christ, our Lord, we are Re-stating and Re-newing our faith covenant to Him based on the biblical charge that He placed on those who have purposed to follow Him. Those who are intent on keeping first things first (see Deut. 5:7).

The most important person who has ever walked on earth stated what He considered to be the most important thing His followers should/could do in obedience to His clear and concise direction. When He said to, *"seek first the Kingdom of God, and His righteousness…"* (Mt. 6:33), He established *Priority #1* for those who consider themselves to be citizens of heaven. (Col. 1:13–14)

"The setting of priority is not a once-and-for-all act. It has to be Re-done frequently. Balances shift. Circumstances change. Moods swing. Is it still God, in fact, with whom I have first of all to do, or is it not? Prayer is the place where the priorities are Re-established."

E. Peterson
(The Re-'s have been added by me for emphasis)

"I've never lived with balance, but I've always liked the notion."
Bruce Cockburn

Selah…pause and consider.

Worship is obedient service manifesting through self-sacrifice. (See Gen. 22:1-5 and Rom. 12:1–2)

A Pondering
JESUS SAID

Here's some of what Jesus had to say about the Kingdom of God and His personal relationship to it:

Why did Jesus come to earth? Jesus said to them, *"I must preach the kingdom of God to the other cities also, for I was sent for this purpose"* (Luke 4:4)

How did He identify His kingdom? Jesus said, *"My kingdom is not of this world."* (Jn. 18:36)

What did He instruct His disciples to pray regarding the kingdom of God? Jesus said, *"Thy Kingdom come, Thy will be done, on earth as it is in heaven..."* (Mt. 6:10)

What did He say was to be priority #1 in the lives of His disciples? Jesus said, *"Seek first the kingdom of God..."* (Mt. 6:33)

How did Jesus say the kingdom of God was intended to apply to the lives of those who follow Him? Jesus said, (Beatitudes Mt.5:1-12 / Sermon on the Mount Mt.5–7).

> "The laws of the Kingdom of God are scattered throughout the New Testament. But there is one compendium of them so profound, comprehensive, explicit, imperial, that it may well be called, The Manifesto of the Kingdom.

It is the so-called "Sermon on the Mount."....the time has now come for Him to enunciate more distinctly the NATURE OF HIS KINGDOM; the CONDITIONS OF CITIZENSHIP in it; and the MODE OF PROPAGATION IT."

The Kingdom: The Emerging Rule of Christ Among Men,
George Dana Boardman

Now, based on the actual words of Jesus quoted above, combined with the insightful comments of Boardman—give some serious thought to 2 Cor. 5:18-21. If you will, you may find the following two points to be of major importance in your spiritual walk, witness, and viable testimony:

Our job description: Ministers of reconciliation

Our job title: Ambassadors of Christ

Our Job
DESCRIPTION AND TITLE

Every follower of Christ has the same job description (Ministry of Reconciliation).
Every follower of Christ has the same job title (Ambassador for Christ)

The kingdom of God is *The Context* for carrying out our ministry and our job description. Without a proper context, ministry may be biblically meaningful in terms of intent, but the content needs a Kingdom context in order to fulfill the dynamics of Eph. 4:11-16. Otherwise ministry itself is merely random in its nature and its application. Meaningful, yes. Fruitful, perhaps. Worthwhile, certainly. But, without a proper context, random nonetheless.

NOTE: A insightful reading source on this topic is *Cosmic Initiative* by Jack Taylor.

A Biblical Perspective
FAITH

"Faith without works is dead."

~Ja. 2:17

And faith without hope doesn't even exist. Why? Because "faith is the substance of things *hoped* for, the evidence of things not seen" (Heb. 11:1). Therefore, if hope isn't present then faith cannot manifest. It takes hope to birth faith.

If you're lacking in faith, or if your faith seems inconsistent, or if you feel you've lost faith altogether—faith isn't the issue. Hope (or the absence of it) is the real problem. Little hope, little faith. Increasing hope, increasing faith.

So, where does hope come from?

"God our Father has given us eternal comfort and good hope by grace."

~2 Thess.2:16 (emphasis mine)

And where does grace come from?

PARTICULAR PONDERING(S)

"Therefore let us draw near with confidence to the throne of grace, so that we may receive mercy and find grace to help in time of need."

~Heb. 4:16

Grace is the unmerited favor of God's empowering presence, enabling us to be who He created us to be, so we can do what He calls us to do.

Excerpts from "The Cycle Of Hope," *Pondering(s) Too* by W. Berry, WordCrafts Press

Here are some interesting and inter-related comments which unpack the topic of faith in a way worth considering:

TRADITION—A good word meaning "the living faith of the dead." Tradition is the embodiment of the Christian faith as contained in the Scriptures through the belief and practice of disciples through the centuries and handed on to present and future generations.

TRADITIONAL—A congregation's or denomination's familiar practices rooted in a given era. What is traditional usually reflects a particular innovation that was embraced as helpful and appropriate in light of the sensibilities and realities of a particular time and place. When the culture changes, the traditional practice may need to be transformed or discarded in order for the living faith of the tradition to move forward unfettered.

TRADITIONALISM—a sad reality: "THE DEAD FAITH OF THE LIVING." When faith is encapsulated in particular forms, words, and routines, without the vitality of vision, compassion, and the Holy Spirit's life-transforming power, the deadly result of traditionalism.

(From: "Contemporary *Discipleship Resources* Worship For The 21st Century" / Daniel Benedict and Craig Miller / '94)

Grace
GIFTED AND REQUESTED

Theologically speaking there are two so-called works of grace presented in Scripture. One is a gift, and one is by request.

"By grace are we saved through faith. It is a gift of God…"
~Eph. 2:8

We can do nothing to earn it. It is a God-given-gift imparted to us at the moment of redemption.

"Therefore let us draw near with confidence (come boldly / KJV) before the throne of grace, so that we may receive mercy and find grace to help in time of need."
~Heb. 4:16

This is grace imparted based on ones willingness to request it—for ourselves and also for others.

Grace is the unmerited favor of God's empowering presence, enabling us to be who He created us to be, so we can do what He calls us to do.

A Pondering
BROKENNESS OR BREAKTHROUGH

I wonder if we'll ever reach a point in time when the so-called *5-Fold Ministry Gifts* of prophets/evangelists/pastors/teachers—along with today's contemporary psalmists—will begin to address those who are *in the house* on the subject of personal and corporate brokenness instead of merely mentioning getting breakthroughs? Brokenness and breakthrough are two entirely different things. In a sense they each may have the same result—freedom. But the way they are approached and outworked are, as I see it, night and day apart.

Brokenness before God implies a state or condition that one brings to Him—not in order to receive personal freedom—but rather to gain personal holiness (or cleanliness). Take some time reading and working through Ps. 51 and you'll likely see what I'm addressing for yourself. As you do, pay close attention to verse 17.

As to securing breakthroughs, they are, in today's church cultures, more about attaining deliverance of some sort. Instead of moving in humility, contrition, and yielded *surrender there seems to me far too much attention directed toward getting out of something rather than pressing into something.

*Worship is obedient service manifesting through self-sacrifice.

Rather than seeking for the Holy Ghost to do something *for* us, perhaps we should revisit the Biblical principle allowing Him to do something *to* us.

Taken/Blessed/Broken/Passed Around (Luke 22:19)—says nothing about getting a *breakthrough* as such. (See also Ps. 51:17 and Isa. 57:15).

FYI: I'm not disavowing the theological concept of breakthroughs as such. I'm only mentioning that the principle of brokenness deserves considerably more attention than it's been getting the last 10-15 years or thereabouts. At least that's how it appears to me.

> *"If My people who are called by My name will humble themselves and pray, seek My face and turn from their wicked ways; then I will hear from heaven, forgive their sin and will heal their land."*
>
> ~2 Chron. 7:14

LAMENT
(Ps. 51)

A broken and a contrite heart, O God, You will not despise
Against You only I have sinned, I have fallen once again
I come to You in emptiness, fill me with Your holiness

CHORUS:

PARTICULAR PONDERING(S)

Create in me a heart that's clean
Draw me to Your side and then
Restore me with Your steadfast love

Have mercy on my wickedness, O God, I seek Your graciousness
Wash away iniquity, remove transgression far from me
I come to You in brokenness, fill me with Your righteousness

REPEAT CHORUS:
(W. Berry / See & Say Songs, BMI)

A Biblical Pov
DIVINE TECH SUPPORT

Speaking scripturally, the *Kingdom of God* is the recommended operating system through which our spiritual PC's were designed to function properly. The Beatitudes provide practical principles and precepts for activating the system (Mt. 5:1-5). Consider them as Start Up prep. The Sermon on the Mount presents the full protocol for understanding how the system is meant to work and how to use it on a regular basis (Mt. 5, 6,7).

An Axiom
The code is The Kingdom
and the Kingdom is the code…

Consider this: *"Seek first the kingdom of God…"* (Mt. 6:33). The word *seek* in the New Testament comes from a Hebrew word in the Old Testament meaning *to worship God*. The word *first* means: Foremost (in time, place, order, or importance); before, at the beginning, chiefly.

Just let that sink in….

Scripturally Speaking
PROFIT AND LOSS

Paul says he had,
"*suffered the loss of all things, and counted them as rubbish so that I may gain Christ…*"
~Phil. 3:8

> "*All the things I once thought were so important are gone from my life. Compared to the high privilege of knowing Christ Jesus as my Master, firsthand, everything I once thought I had going for me is insignificant—dog dung. I've dumped it all in the trash so that I could embrace Christ and be embraced my Him.*"
> ~Phil. 3:8 (MSG)

When Paul makes that statement, he's speaking of *all* things temporal being counted as worthless, pointless, and of no real lasting value *compared* to the worth of eternal things living in/for/with Christ Jesus.

The term "all things" is speaking of every success or failure, each dream promised—fulfilled or unfilled (See Heb. 11:37-39). Everything considered to be of value among humankind.

All evaluated as insignificant in matters regarding an intimate union with the Lord of lords.

In light of such a Biblical confession as that on Paul's part, how do we treasure our personal and corporate relationships with our Lord and Savior?

Selah...pause and consider.

Spiritual Engagement
PURPOSED-PRO-ACTIVITY

Serving in the Kingdom of God is not a vicarious experience. Rather, it requires personal participation. As a minister of reconciliation (job description) and as an ambassador for Christ (job title). See 2 Cor. 5:18-21.

Scripturally Speaking
TWO KINDS OF HOPE

"If we have hope in this world only, we are of all men most miserable."
~1 Cor. 15:19 (KJV)

"If all we get out of Christ is a little inspiration for a few short years, we're a pretty sorry lot."
~1 Cor. 15:19 (MSG)

In the verse above, Paul is addressing two specific types of hope. One is temporal—earth based, bound by time—the other is eternal—based on the hereafter, unrestricted by time and worldly circumstances.

In the text it seems clear to me that Paul considers access to the temporal type of hope as a given in the lives of those who have lived here, those who are living here now, and those who'll live here later. He's not really addressing that type of hope as such, except to acknowledge that it exists.

The real focus of his comments is directed toward those who are followers of Christ, and having access to the eternal type of hope, choose to focus their hope only on the earth-bound type. He says that he views people such as that as being "most miserable." (KJV)

Bear in mind that those he's addressing are—apparently—followers of Christ. That being the case, Paul is stating that from among believers who are redeemed, born again, and bound for heaven some can still live lives that are less that fulfilling; less than abundant. (See Jn. 10:10b).

If we live out our days with our hope fixed only on things that take place on the planet, we will likely do so with a sorrowful and sad disregard for the "Blessed Hope." (Titus 2:13)

Ponder that for a while…

A Biblical Perspective
FAITH AND/OR TRUST

There's a huge difference in having faith to believe that God will answer the prayers you pray and having enough trust in His Sovereignty to believe that He can do anything He wants to do with your prayers—answered or not.

"Yet thought He slay me, still will I trust Him."
~Job 13:15

IN HIS HANDS

Your prayers are never yours alone
You offer them to God, and they become His own
And then He fashions them to fit, into His perfect plan
Your prayers are not your own, once they're in His hands

Your dreams don't belong to you
They're part of Father's heart, even when they don't come true
You have still been blessed to share, in things that He has planned
Your dreams are never yours alone, once they're in His hands

PARTICULAR PONDERING(S)

Your life, it is a gift from God, ordered in His care
Through mercy, grace, and love
And when, when you give your life to Him
With all the praise you can
Your life becomes His own, once you're in hands
                              (W. Berry / See & Say Songs, BMI)

A Biblical Perspective
INTERNAL INTAKE AND SPIRITUAL HEALTH

If our personal daily intake consists of distractive entertainment, disruptive disunity, chaotic consideration, harbored hatred, blind bigotry, red vs. blue stuff, gross greed, pet perversions, outright obstinance, stubbornness, cultural conformity, self-vindication, indulged entitlements, and the like—then our spiritual health is at risk. Why? Because each of those subjects has its root base in *sin*. They contain no redemptive components.

If that's the case, as followers of Christ, we are not operating out of Col. 3:1-3 (MSG) which says:

> *So if you're serious about living this new resurrection life with Christ, act like it. Pursue the things over which Christ presides. Don't shuffle along, eyes to the ground, absorbed with the things right in front of you. Look up, and be alert to what is going on around Christ—that's where the action is. See things from his perspective. Your old life is dead. Your new life, which is your real life—even though invisible to spectators—is with Christ in God. He is your life. When Christ (your real life, remember) shows up again on this earth, you'll show up, too—the real you, the glorious you.*

PARTICULAR PONDERING(S)

Meanwhile, be content with obscurity, like Christ."
*See also Rom. 12:1–2 (MSG)

In order for our intake to be Biblically based, perhaps we could consider a change in our diets to include this:

"Don't fret or worry. Instead of worrying, pray. Let petitions and praises shape your worries into prayers, letting God know your concerns. Before you know it, a sense of God's wholeness, everything coming together for good, will come and settle you down. It's wonderful what happens when Christ displaces worry at the center of your life. Summing it all up, friends, I'd say you'll do best by filling your minds and meditating on things true, noble, reputable, authentic, compelling, gracious—the best, not the worst; the beautiful, not the ugly; things to praise, not things to curse. Put into practice what you learned from me, what you heard and saw and realized. Do that, and God, who makes everything work together, will work you into his most excellent harmonies."
~Phil. 4:6-9 (MSG)

We could also add in something the Sovereign God suggested:

If My people who are called by My name humble themselves and pray and seek My face and turn from their wicked ways, then I will hear from heaven, will forgive their sin and will heal their land."
~2 Chron. 7:14

Think of it as spiritual fiber…

A Pondering
KINGDOM PONDERING(S)

"The heart of Jesus is the capitol of God's kingdom. That is not a philosophical concept taught by a philosophical rabbi. It is something to live for and to die for; Jesus was a teacher—but he was also the Redeemer, heading the greatest movement that ever struck our planet, the kingdom of God."

~E. Stanley Jones

T his…

"Yet, my brothers, I do not consider myself to have 'arrived,' spiritually, nor do I consider myself already perfect. But I keep going on, grasping ever more firmly that purpose for which Christ grasped me. My brothers, I do not consider myself to have fully grasped it even now. But I do concentrate on this: I leave the past behind and with hands outstretched to whatever lies ahead I go straight for the goal—my reward the honor of being called by God in Christ."

~Phil. 3:12-14 (Phillips)

PARTICULAR PONDERING(S)

That prompted this…

I'm lookin' forward to the future, there's no point in lookin' back
What's already come is over and done, I can't do a thing about that
I'm steppin' in to my destiny, I'm excited 'bout what I'll see
I hear tomorrow callin' me
(And) The future looks bright ahead…

A Pondering
WORD UP

I learned a new word today: *men·da·cious*
ADJECTIVE
not telling the truth; lying.
"mendacious propaganda"
synonyms:
lying; untruthful; dishonest; deceitful; false; dissembling; insincere; disingenuous; hypocritical; fraudulent; double-dealing; two-faced; Janus-faced; two-timing; duplicitous; perjured; perfidious; untrue; fictitious; falsified; fabricated; fallacious; invented; made up; hollow; economical with the truth; terminologically inexact; unveracious

It's a heavy word, weighted down by misrepresentation and misbehavior.

"Let your statement be, 'Yes, yes' or 'No, no'; anything beyond that is of evil."

~Mt. 5:37

A Pondering
KINGDOM CONSIDERATIONS

"Under the Old Covenant, Isa. 61:1–2 gives us the context for the prophetic words which addressed the pending (and eternal) ministry of Jesus. Then, in Luke 4:18–19, Jesus quotes the very same passage as the context for His personal ministry *"on earth as it is in heaven"* under the New Covenant.

Both of those examples are directly and specifically related to the Kingdom of God. Here's how:

Now note the redemptions to be brought with the coming of the Kingdom. Did redemption ever go into more important and more creative channels? God's revolution which is God's kingdom, brought redemption into:

- The economic—good news to the poor
- The social and political—release to the captives
- The physical—recovery of sight to the blind
- The moral and spiritual—to strengthen with forgiveness those who are being bruised

A fresh world beginning on the basis of equality of opportunity for all—the Lord's year of jubilee. Here was a revolution that is to remake the economic, the social and political, the physical, the moral and spiritual, and the total structure of life."

~E. Stanley Jones

A Pondering
ANOTHER KINGDOM PONDERING

(Priority #1)

"I am seeking. I am striving. I am in it with all my heart."
~Vincent van Gogh

This is a quote from E. Stanley Jones, in his book *The Unshakable Kingdom And The Unchanging Person*, published in 1972. It provides insight as to why (and how) the church-at-large has become so seemingly irrelevant to so many people in today's culture.

"Jesus devoted a whole chapter to the kingdom of God (see Mt. 13), and in the midst of it he used the phrase, a disciple of the kingdom of God. This was illuminating and revealing. He had called them to be his disciples, and he was to call them to make all nations his disciples, but here he went further and called his disciples to be 'disciples of the kingdom of God.' Here he put together these two things and made them one—to be his disciple was to be a disciple of the kingdom of God. To be his disciple was to be a disciple of his message, the Kingdom. He taught them many things, but he never asked his disciples to be disciples to anything except himself—nothing else, except the Kingdom. He identified himself and the Kingdom so completely that to be a disciple of one was to be a disciple of the other. But here what God has joined together man has put asunder. We have called men to be disciples of Jesus, but not disciples of the kingdom of God—to take the King but not his kingdom. This has weakened the impact of Jesus upon the world. It is a personal relation of a person to a Person, but not a relationship with the order embodied in that Person. This was a vital loss, for the order was to be the life program of the disciple. Nothing can be compared with that loss, and nothing can be compared to the gain when we become disciples to the Kingdom."

Consider Col. 1:13 which states,

"For He rescued us from the domain of darkness and transferred us to the kingdom of His beloved Son, in whom we have redemption, the forgiveness of sins."

If that verse is true, and it is, then it should follow that those who are *"in Christ"* (Col. 3:1-3) would live as if they are citizens of God's kingdom. Do we?

Selah…pause and consider.

A Biblical Perspective
THE HUMAN CONDITION

"We see that one act of sin exposed the whole race of men to God's judgment and condemnation…"
~Rom. 5:18–19 (Phillips)

The Fall of humankind came to pass through the sin of one man. The curse of sin is the endless manifestation of death, which is resident in the DNA of every person who has ever lived, is living now, or will live in the future. (Rom. 3:23)

In 1950 there were approximately three billion people on earth. In 2019, just 60 years later, there are some seven billion plus inhabiting the same space. As a result, the rising level of sin on the planet is considerably higher than it's ever been. Do you see where I'm going with this?

The real problem in our collective human condition isn't politics or ecology—global warming, etc. Nor is it our cultural disposition, mores, immigration, the economy, or our lack of moral, religious, or spiritual values. Our problem is *sin*—individual and collective: Our lack of acknowledgement of it. Our need to properly address it, and the process by which it is dealt with.

> *"...so one act of perfect righteousness presents all men freely acquitted in the sight of God. One man's disobedience placed all men under the threat of condemnation, but one man's obedience has the power to present all men righteous before God."*
>
> ~Rom. 5:20–21 (Phillips)

Selah…pause and consider.

A Pondering
LISTENING FOR SILENCE

I keep seeing videos links online of musicians from about 30 years of age, down to around 10 or so. Many of them are clearly talented on their instruments. But most, if not all of them, seem to have three things in common. What they play is full of flash, not style. Flash and style are not the same thing. One is based on form, the other is based on substance.

How they play is frenetic, hyper, with lots of notes, leaving very little room for air in between.

Generally speaking, they mostly play alone without any others accompanying them.

I wonder who'll teach them what not to play. By that I'm referring to the art of knowing what to leave out.

Making music just ain't what it used to be...

> *"Sometimes you can hear the spirit whispering to you*
> *But, if God stays silent, what else can you do*
> *Except listen to the silence*
> *If you ever did, you'd surely see*
> *That God won't be reduced to an ideology..."*
> ~B. Cockburn

A Biblical Perspective
LIFE AND LIFESTYLE

As followers of Christ, we cannot (or should not) think we can say or do whatever we desire. Here's why:

> *"Whatever you do in word or deed, do all in the name of the Lord Jesus, giving thanks through Him to God the Father."*
> ~Col. 3:17

There are dozens, perhaps hundreds of verses in Scripture which address that topic. However, I think that one singular text pretty much covers it.
Don't you?
https://focusmagazine.org/peace-with-all-men.php
Also see Heb. 12:14.

A Pondering
THE Rx FOR CURING NATIONALIZED RELIGION(s)

> *"Of the increase of his government and of peace there shall be no end, on the throne of David, and on his kingdom, to establish it, and to uphold it with justice and with righteousness from that time on, even forever. The zeal of the LORD of hosts will perform this."*
>
> ~Isa. 9:7 (NHEB)

Considering that the kingdom of God is eternal (and it is), with no beginning middle, or end, then perhaps we should each ask ourselves this following question:

If the country which we consider as our homeland were to no longer exist, would God's kingdom still be active, accessible, and expanding?

Selah…pause and consider.

SPOILER ALERT: Christianity and Capitalism are not synonyms. Neither are Patriotism and Nationalism.

A Perspective
ON PROSE

In '65, this song was a sort of anthem for those between their late teens and late 20s. The content was perhaps a little mean-spirited, as was the era and the intent. Back in those daze it was directed at the older generation—the over 30s.

Oddly, and interestingly, today it now applies when directed toward those who are under 30, passed down from those who are over 60. I'm not sure if that qualifies it as a *classic*. But I am sure that it's a hoot just to consider the shelf-life of so called pop-culture-social-commentary. As is said now and then, what goes around, comes around. *Peace out!*

MY GENERATION" (The Who)
https://www.youtube.com/watch?v=uswXI4fDYrM

Cause: *"…because they abandoned the covenant of the LORD their God and bowed in worship to other gods and served them."*
~Jer. 22:9 (CSB)

Effect: Just look around…

POV
LIVING IN CRAZY-DAZE

This is the actual copy taken from the back wrapper of a candy bar I just ate. And I quote…

"In choosing this chocolate bar, you join us in elevating the care of both people and planet.
Our chocolate is extra delicious because we support training and education which enables farmers to produce higher quality cocoa. We pay farmers quality premiums that far exceed fair trade premiums, empowering them to invest in regenerative farming practices which renew and revitalize their farms."

People—it's a chocolate candy bar!

I can't even…

POV
A BOOMER'S POV

One of the surest ways of confirming that you've grown old is to see names and photos of people of reputation, honor, power, fame, fortune, who are known for being culturally important popping up everywhere—and having no idea who they are.

Those of you who are laughing at this, just you wait.

A Pondering
CHANNELING GRACE

"Let us, therefore, come boldly unto the throne of his grace, that we may obtain mercy and find grace to help in time of need."
~Heb. 4:16 (JUB)

There are two basic ways to relate to that verse as I read it. One is to consider appropriating grace for ourselves in our time of need. That is certainly a correct way of understanding the text. Many translations render it that way. However, I see nothing in the text that limits or restricts our ability to receive grace for ourselves alone.

What if we were to approach the throne of grace with two intentions:
- To receive grace for ourselves and our own needs
- To receive grace on behalf of others in order to make it available to them in their times of need

If you were to decide to begin applying both reasons for securing grace—for yourself and for others—you'd do well to remember this: The grace you pass along isn't yours, it's God's. You are only a channel for it to flow through.

Grace is the unmerited favor of God's empowering presence, enabling me to be who He created me to be, so I can do what He calls me to do. (Wayne-speak)

A Biblical Perspective
KINGDOM STUFF

When Jesus began His ministry on earth, He didn't do so by starting a new religion called Christianity. That term didn't even exist till after He had things up and runnin'. Rather, He came proclaiming—introducing and modeling—an entirely new way of living. That new lifestyle was to be carried out within a wholly/holy "other" context of life called the Kingdom of God.

The components—principles and precepts—of that Kingdom were specially addressed when He presented the Beatitudes (Mt. 5:1-11). Those components were contained in and explained in the protocol presented in the Sermon on the Mount (Mt. 5-7).

Those same principles, and precepts, along with the protocol, are as applicable today as they were when Christ first spoke them. They should be adhered to by each and every person who considers themselves to be followers of Christ: citizens of God's kingdom, ministers of reconciliation, and ambassadors for Christ. (See 2 Cor. 5:18-21.)

Selah...pause and consider.

A Pondering
GENERATIONAL UNITY

"When the builders laid the foundation of the temple of the LORD, the priests in their vestments and with trumpets, and the Levites (the sons of Asaph) with cymbals, took their places to praise the LORD, as prescribed by David king of Israel. With praise and thanksgiving they sang to the LORD: 'He is good; his love toward Israel endures forever.' And [all] the people gave a great shout of praise to the LORD, because the foundation of the house of the LORD was laid. But many of the older priests and Levites and family heads, who had seen the former temple, wept aloud when they saw the foundation of this temple being laid, while many others shouted for joy. No one could distinguish the sound of the shouts of joy from the sound of weeping, because the people made so much noise. And the sound was heard far away."

~Ezra 3:10-13

There's a valuable point of connection in that passage which is easily misunderstood or perhaps overlooked entirely. The weeping of the old men—older generation—was based on what *they* had personally experienced. It was an emotional response rooted in *their* memory. It was not intended as some sort of criticism or condescending indictment of the younger generation. That would have been pointless since they had not shared in that former experience—since they were not living back then. In other words, the older were moved to tears at their remembrance of times past, as the younger were celebrating the current event which was taking place.

The text says that *"the people could not distinguish the sound of the shout of joy from the sound of the weeping of the people."* Their response was collective, congregational, corporate. They offered one unified action—*together*.

Those of the older generations in the church should attempt to learn how to enter into the celebrations of the younger. And, the younger generations should try to learn how to accept, and honor, the historical realities that those who came before them carry in their hearts and minds. *"Behold how good and pleasant it is...."* (Ps. 133:1)

LEAD ME
(Ps. 16:11, 27:11 / 119:33-40)

Lead me in the path of the righteous
For Your name's sake, for Your name's sake
Lead me in the way everlasting
For the glory of Your kingdom
O Lord, my God

'Cause I don't wanna lose my way
And wind up in the wilderness
Hear this prayer I pray

GENERATIONAL UNITY

Order my steps upright
I don't wanna lose my way
And wind up in the wilderness
Guide my steps each day
Lead me to the Light

(W. Berry / See & Say Songs, BMI)

A Pondering
PONDERING WORSHIP

It seems to me that worship is now most commonly considered to be an "experience". However, it is, Biblically speaking, a lifestyle.

> *"So here's what I want you to do, God helping you: Take your everyday, ordinary life—your sleeping, eating, going-to-work, and walking-around life—and place it before God as an *offering."*
>
> –Rom. 12:1 (MSG)

*"living sacrifice" in the KJV / "spiritual service of worship" in the NASB

Worship is rooted in self-denial, in order for the person, place, or thing being worshiped to receive honor, exaltation, or praise. The first mention of worship is presented/modeled in Scripture in Gen. 22:5 which says, *"Then Abraham said to his young men, 'Stay here with the donkey; I and the boy will go over there and worship and come again to you.'"*

According to that text, the first worshipper was Abraham. But, his act of worship through obedient sacrifice wasn't his alone. There were two gathered. Isaac was joined with him in worship through his own obedient act of self-sacrifice.

My current working definition of worship is this:

Worship is obedient service manifesting through self-sacrifice.

Selah…pause and consider.

A Pondering
PONDERING POWER

The power to live as a witness for the kingdom in testimony and service as a *"living sacrifice"* (Rom. 12:1–2) is released and manifested—first and foremost—through God's presence:

> *"But you will receive power after the Holy Spirit comes to you. Then you will be my witnesses to testify about me in Jerusalem, throughout Judea and Samaria, and to the ends of the earth."*
> ~Acts 1:8 (GOD'S WORD)

Note that the verse says that *presence* precedes *power*. Without a keen awareness of presence, any power that's produced is, or should be, at the very least, questionable. If the power to shake things up in the advancement of God's kingdom comes from any source besides Presence, it would likely be a good idea to refrain from appropriating and applying it for use altogether.

"And when they had prayed, the place was shaken where they

were assembled together; and they were all filled with the Holy Spirit, and they spoke the word of God with boldness."
~Acts 4:31 (JUB)

Here's a worthwhile read on the subject of power (it's proper and improper usage)…

The Way of the Dragon or the Way of the Lamb: Searching for Jesus' Path of Power in a Church that Has Abandoned It, by Kyle Strobel

A Pondering
GENERATIONAL LINKAGE

The process through which the truths of God's Word (principles, precepts, laws, commandments, etc.) are passed along to the generations yet to come is presented clearly in the passage below.

> *"From my childhood you've been my teacher, and I'm still telling everyone of your miracle-wonders! God, now that I'm old and gray, don't walk away. Give me grace to demonstrate to the next generation all your mighty miracles and your excitement, to show them your magnificent power!"*
> ~Ps. 71:17–18 (TPT)

Notice the phrase which says, "give me *grace." That's an important key to unlocking how such a process is to be implemented.

*Grace is the unmerited favor of God's empowering presence, enabling me to be who He created me to be, so I can do what He calls me to do.

The one thing that activates what's addressed/encouraged in the text is grace, for it provides the hope necessary to carry out the charge through faith. Grace imparts hope (2 Thess. 2:16 and 1 Pet. 1:13), hope births faith (Heb. 11:1), and faith enables the followers of Christ to walk out their beliefs in ways which can then manifest to those coming up behind them. That is the Biblical blueprint for how generational linkage is to take place from one era to the next. It's the bridge that spans the cavern between one generation of believers and the next. Without that bridge in place, a huge chasm separates the one from the other, creating a spiritual *generation gap* instead of a collective-corporate-unity.

Carrying out the task at hand isn't based on how the information is received by those it's given to. The fundamental charge is to those who can/will pass such truth(s) along. That's their responsibility. How it's received—or rejected—isn't part of the charge itself. The appropriation isn't predicated on its distribution. The mandate is to pass it along. Thereafter, the uptake is between the recipients and the Holy Ghost.

There's an old saying which applies here: You can lead a horse to water, but you can't make him drink.

The principle that the process is grounded upon is found in Ezek. 33:7-9 (MSG) which states,

> *"You, son of man, are the watchman. I've made you a watchman for Israel. The minute you hear a message from me, warn them. If I say to the wicked, 'Wicked man, wicked woman, you're on the fast track to death!' and you don't speak up and warn the wicked to change their ways, the wicked will die unwarned in their sins and I'll hold you responsible for their bloodshed. But if you warn the wicked to change their ways and they don't do it, they'll die in their sins well-warned and at least you will have saved your own life."*

The liability for passing along Scriptural values lies with those who have them. That principle has as a sub-set-precept—that of seed sowing. Those who sow seed aren't directly responsible for how the seed grows, or if it grows at all. The sole purpose of sowing seed is seeing to it that it is, in fact, sown whenever and wherever that can be done. The results of the sowing can only manifest to the degree that seed has been distributed over and into the soil.

For that reason, it is vital that the Word is resident and active (internalized) in those who are responsible for passing it along. The personal witness of Word-truth is directly imparted through the testimony (lifestyle) of those who are to represent it to those who are under their charge so to speak. At least that's how the process of connectivity is to take place as I understand it.

There's another passage that echoes (resonates) with what I've just shared.

> *"He planted a witness in Jacob, set his Word firmly in Israel, then commanded our parents to teach it to their children so the next generation would know, and all the generations to come—know the truth and tell the stories so their children can trust in God, never forget the works of God but keep his commands to the letter."*
>
> ~Ps. 78:5-7 (MSG)

The text continues with the image of God Himself doing the seed sowing, and that planting then is identified as being a witness in and of itself. That is to say that the Word-Seed becomes a witness and that witness in turn becomes a testimonial when it's given by the person in which the Word has taken root and produced fruit in the life of the carrier.

It goes on to say that it is the job of the parents to pass along what they know to their children. Not the school system—Christian or otherwise. Not the government—Democratic or otherwise. Not the culture—Kingdom or otherwise. Biblically speaking, it is the task of those who are raising children to pass along Bible-based truths (stories). Why?

"So their children can trust in God, never forget the words of God but keep His commands to the letter."

I'll say no more about that here. The Word can/will speak for itself.

Don't shout me down!

A Biblical POV
WINE AND WINESKINS

During our most recent trip to Africa, a teaching from Bishop Joseph Garlington blew us away. The insight he shared set the stage for a revelation that I will be processing for some time to come.

Here's what he said in part regarding the parable of the "new wineskin" (Luke 5:36-39).

When that parable is considered, we mistakenly think that the new skin that's needed to hold the new wine is to be fashioned from a completely different skin to replace the old one. Scripturally speaking that is not the case—at least not completely. Here's why: The word *new* in the Greek language can also be understood (defined) as *fresh*—or, if you will, *made new*. To do so there is a process that has to be followed.

The process of refreshing an old skin so that it can then contain the new wine is as follows:

First, the skin has to be soaked—saturated—with clean, fresh water. Then, while it is still wet—drenched—any places that are still hard, brittle, or incapable of expanding—stretching—are beaten with a rock in order to soften any areas that the soaking has not penetrated. The third step is to take the skin and re-soak it with fresh oil, rubbing it by hand until it has been completely softened—repristinated.

That process is of major importance as it relates to how generational connections are to be made and maintained as the body of Christ moves from one season of cultural interaction into the one to come. (See Ps. 71:18 and Ps. 78:58.)

A study of interest can perhaps be considered from Ps. 51:1–2 {Blot: To beat on stone / Wash: To soak in a cleansing bath / Cleanse: To hammer out spots with a wooden mallet}

Keep this in mind. How one handles revelation should be based on a process: Revelation to Transformation to Impartation

Perhaps I'll unpack that process at another point in time.

MY EYES ARE DRY

My eyes are dry, my faith is old
My heart is hard, my prayers are cold
And I know how I ought to be Alive to You and dead to me
Oh what can be done for an old heart like mine
Soften it up with oil and wine
The oil is You, Your Spirit of love
Please wash me anew in the wine of Your blood
(Keith & Melody Green, Universal Music Publishing Group used by permission)

"Every Generation, demands a demonstration, of the church of Jesus, relevant to its time. I am determined to be part of that generation."

~Helena Barrington and Peter Morgan, '92

"...every scribe who has become a disciple of the kingdom of

PARTICULAR PONDERING(S)

heaven is like the head of a household, who brings out of his treasure things new and old."
~Mt. 13:52

"But as for me, I trust in You, O Lord, I say, 'You are my God.' My times are in Your hand..."
~Ps. 31:14-15a

"Whatever you do in word or deed, do it all in the name of the Lord Jesus, giving thanks through Him to God the Father."
~Col. 3:17

A Pondering
THY KINGDOM COME, THY WILL BE DONE

God's kingdom provides *the* context in which *all* the aspects of His divine and eternal plan can be expressed, experienced, and expanded. It gives us the *why, what,* and *how* of a Biblically-based life:
- Why is there a kingdom? It is God's Sovereign will.
- What is the kingdom? It is *the context* for expressing God's Sovereign will.
- How does the kingdom work? It functions in accordance with God's Sovereign will, explained in an overview in the Beatitudes and in detail in the Sermon on the Mount

A kingdom requires a Ruler, those being ruled, and rules. For those who consider themselves to be followers of Christ, this kingdom business is important. Consider this: When the disciples needed direction regarding prayer, Jesus gave them a blueprint to work from.

"And then, when you pray, don't be like the play-actors. They love to stand and pray in the synagogues and at street-corners so that people may see them at it. Believe me, they have had all the reward they are going to get. But when you pray, go

into your own room, shut your door and pray to your Father privately. Your Father who sees all private things will reward you. And when you pray don't rattle off long prayers like the pagans who think they will be heard because they use so many words. Don't be like them. After all, God, who is your Father, knows your needs before you ask him. Pray then like this—'Our Heavenly Father, may your name be honored; May your kingdom come, and your will be done on earth as it is in heaven. Give us this day the bread we need, Forgive us what we owe to you, as we have also forgiven those who owe anything to us. Keep us clear of temptation, and save us from evil.'"

~Mt. 6:9-13 (Phillips)

He didn't give it to them for repetition only. It was to be put into practice. (See Col. 3:17)

Selah…pause and consider.

A Pondering
A NEW YEAR TESTIMONAL

The first known attribute of God's character and nature that He chose to reveal to humankind was creativity (Gen. 1:1). In accordance with that Biblically-based fact, I offer up the following testimony. (See Col. 3:17.)

In the Fall of 2016, I published my first book titled, *PONDERING(S)*. Then, with the help of several dear friends, associates, resource contributors, and kingdom cohorts, I began developing a CD project for release in the summer of 2017. *Journey Mercies* became a sonic reality along with a "live" concert DVD that Fall. Following that, work started on a new manuscript entitled *PONDERING(S) TOO*. While it was in the drafting stage, two other projects took shape. One is a collection of 29 previously unheard and unreleased song demos, circa '72-'74 called *Detour (A Prodigal's Chronicles)*. The other is a Wayne Berry YouTube channel with links to all of my past recordings, along with songs of mine recorded by other artists which were available for link-ups, as well as any other projects (audio and/or video) that I've taken part in over the last 50+ years.

The restoration and renewal process continues in my life

through the sanctifying work of the Holy Ghost, the intercession of Christ Jesus, and the gracious lovingkindness of the One True God. Self-achievement should not be considered as the life goal of a follower of Christ. Self-sacrifice should. Worship is obedient service manifesting through self-sacrifice. (See Gen. 22:1-5 and Rom. 12:1.)

"The lines have fallen to me in pleasant places."

~Ps. 16:6

Both books and *Journey Mercies* and *Detour* are available are available from fine online and brick 'n' mortar stores worldwide. All profits go directly toward funding mission sojourns on the African continent through Outbound Ministries International.

Abandoning Ourselves To
THE GOODNESS AND GRACE OF OUR FATHER

Whom have I in heaven but you? And earth has nothing I desire besides you. My flesh and my heart may fail, but God is the strength of my heart and my portion forever.
~Ps. 73:25-26

"Heavenly Father, as we ponder the impassioned declaration of the Psalmist, we also cry out, "Us too, Lord, us too!" May we live by the mathematics of mercy—faith calculating your unparalleled worth in a world of fool's gold and temporal pleasures.

Grant us the perspective of eternity, that we might live our days with heaven's hope and its matchless joys in view. Keep us gospel-sane—thinking with the mind of Christ, reasoning by the riches of grace, and worshipping you in Spirit and truth.

Father, give us more satisfaction in yourself than in any story, situation, or circumstance we might choose for ourselves. Thank you for giving us many gifts to enjoy, but we want you to be the most gratifying feast of hearts—our portion and passion, our treasure and inheritance. By your Holy Spirit, make it so. Make it more true and real to us than ever before.

Forgive us for our ingratitude and envy, our fears and lack of trust. Free us from every expression of entitlement and demandingness. Heal our gospel-amnesia, Father. We too easily forget that we are your children of delight; your daughters and sons of grace; those you've hidden in Christ, sealed for eternity, and rejoice over with singing.

Oh, blessed, loving, and merciful Father, we worship and adore you today, and forever. So very Amen we pray, in Jesus' exalted and glorious name."

~Scotty Smith
Sunday, November 11, 2018

"It appears that our strict "belief systems" (which are different in each group) has blinded us to many of the mysteries of Scripture. The beliefs I held in my youth are different from the beliefs I hold today. The more I learn the more I realize how little I understand the mystery. Harvey Cox rightly makes a distinction between beliefs and faith. "We can believe something to be true without it making much difference to us, but we place our faith only in something that is vital for the way we live," he wrote. If it doesn't affect our life outreach, we don't really believe it."

~Fount Shults

A Personal POV
20/20 VISION

Sunglasses with Polarized lenses provide a way to see the world with less harmful glare. However, if the lenses get scratched up or cracked, polarization won't help with the distortion. Such is the case considering the difference between living with a *World-View* as opposed to a *Biblical-World-View*. One sees life on earth as it appears to be while the other enables us to see it as it really is. That's an *"on earth as it is in heaven"* perspective. Just because we can't see something, doesn't mean it's not there. (2 Kings 6:17)

Do you see what I'm sayin'?

A Biblical POV
WORSHIP

Consider this: Gen. 22:5 is the first time the word *worship* is presented in Scripture. In its context, it has to do with Abraham offering himself in obedience to Jehovah through the potential death of his only son. Then, in Job 1:20, the word *worshipped* is used to explain how Job responded just after he'd received the news that all of his children had been tragically killed.

The words *worship* and *worshipped* have the same basic meaning in Hebrew: To depress or prostrate (in homage to royalty or God). To bow (the self), to crouch or fall down. To show reverence toward. To make to stoop.

Then, in Rom. 12:1, Paul tells us we should, "present our bodies (ourselves) as living sacrifices, acceptable to God, which is our spiritual *service of worship*." That directly links the obedient service of self-sacrifice mentioned in the story of both Abraham and Job, with the New Testament directive of presenting ourselves—our very being—to God as a live offering of worship.

*The KJV uses the phrase "reasonable service". The word *service* there means ministration to God (i.e. worship—as in worship of God)

Ponder on that for a while…

WORSHIP

"Religion has often suffered from the tendency to become parochial, self-indulgent, self-seeking…it has often done more to canonize prejudices than to wrestle for truth; to petrify the sacred than to sanctify the secular."
~Abraham Heschel

Nothing worth having comes without some kind of fight
You've got to kick at the darkness 'til it bleeds daylight.
Lovers In A Dangerous Time, B. Cockburn,
Golden Mountain Music Corp, Used by permission

A Pondering
WORD PICTURES

Here's a beautiful example of how literalism and metaphor can meld together into a perfect picture of purposed prose:

"For there is hope for a tree, when it is cut down, that it will sprout again, and its shoots will not fail. Though its roots grow old in the ground and its stump dies in the dry soil, at the scent of water it will flourish and put forth sprigs like a plant." \

–Job 14:7-9

A Pondering
PROPHETIC FULFILLMENT

"…though it tarry, wait for it."
~Hab. 2:3

"For those who live in Jerusalem and their rulers, because they did not recognize him nor understand the utterances of the prophets, which are read every Sabbath, fulfilled them by condemning him. And though they found in him no guilt worthy of death, they asked Pilate to have him executed. And when they had carried out all that was written of him, they took him down from the tree and laid him in a tomb. But God raised him from the dead, and for many days he appeared to those who had come up with him from Galilee to Jerusalem, who are now his witnesses to the people. And we bring you the good news that what God promised to the fathers, this he has fulfilled to us their children by raising Jesus, as also it is written in the second Psalm, "'You are my Son, today I have begotten you.'"
~Acts 13:27-33 (ESV

Notice these phrases:
"fulfilled them (the prophets) by condemning Him"
"they asked Pilate to have Him executed"

"But God raised Him from the dead"
"…what God promised to the fathers…"
"…this He has fulfilled"
"…by raising Jesus, as also it is written in the second Psalm"

In Summary: Condemning Christ to death was the way that the prophets' words were fulfilled. That was done when the Father raised Jesus from the dead. Which in turn fulfilled Ps. 2 which had been uttered centuries prior to the Savior being born. The process of prophetic fulfillment can take a very, very long time—even centuries. And the process can be filled with pain and loss in its unfolding.

Selah…pause and consider.

A Biblical POV
REPENTANCE

"...repentance that leads to life."

~Acts 11:18

Repentance isn't just something we do after we've confessed our sin(s). The basic definition has to do with changing the way we think. In other words, it involves rethinking, or revising, how our thought processes work.

Repentance is a way of life based on our personal and/or corporate Biblically-based understanding of Scripture and how we apply it as citizens and representatives of God's kingdom.

Biblically speaking, repentance always comes *after* conviction and *confession. That is to say, repentance is the third step toward restoration and renewal.

*Confession can be addressed horizontally—toward those who have been wronged in some way by our actions. It can also be addressed vertically toward God—whom we wrong anytime we wrong others. It can also involve both directions —horizontal as well as vertical.

"The entrance into the Kingdom is through the panging pains of repentance crashing into a man's respectable goodness…the new life (in Christ) will manifest itself in conscious repentance and unconscious holiness, never the other way around."

~O. Chambers (clarification added)

A Pondering
CONSIDERING BLESSEDNESS

Commenting on the beatitude which says, *"Blessed are the meek for they shall inherit the earth"* (Mt. 5:5), George Boardman had this to say in 1899:

"Beware, my countrymen, how you allow yourselves to be beguiled into territorial expansion by the blustering talk about the certainty of American domination or 'manifest destiny.' Earth's majesties are no match for the King's meek ones."

Boardman continues stating, *"Blessed are those who hunger and thirst after righteousness..."* (Mt. 5:6)

"All souls are made to crave. We crave for husks as well as for manna. Righteousness is the only food that can meet this craving—the righteousness of actual character, the righteousness of doing the King's will personally, consciously, joyously; the righteousness of personal perfectness, even as our heavenly Father is perfect: this is the righteousness, and this only, which can satisfy the soul's true hunger."

Then he adds, *"...for they shall be filled."*

"The righteous soul's growing volume ever demands a growing volume of food; and the hunger for any given stage will be duly met at that stage. Demand and supply, so disproportioned in this world's economics, are correlatives in the Kingdom of God."

Stunning insights!

A Pondering
ON EARTH AS IT IS IN HEAVEN

In heaven—in eternity—the Trinity is relationally unified—3 in 1. As followers of Christ we have a specific job to do: We are charged with extending the "ministry of reconciliation" to *all* humankind as the Father did in and through the Son (See 2 Cor. 5:18). To accomplish that, we're given a specific job title. We are to serve God's kingdom as ambassadors for Christ (See 2 Cor. 5:20).

The way that works out is explained in Rom. 12:1–2 (MSG);

"So here's what I want you to do, God helping you: Take your everyday, ordinary life—your sleeping, eating, going-to-work, and walking-around life—and place it before God as an offering. Embracing what God does for you is the best thing you can do for him. Don't become so well-adjusted to your culture that you fit into it without even thinking. Instead, fix your attention on God. You'll be changed from the inside out. Readily recognize what he wants from you, and quickly respond to it. Unlike the culture around you, always dragging you down to its level of immaturity, God brings the best out of you, develops well-formed maturity in you."

That passage is echoed in Col. 3:17 (MSG) stating,

"Let every detail in your lives – words, actions, whatever – be done in the name of the Master, Jesus, thanking God the Father every step of the way."

That's how obedient service takes place. There's a name for that—*worship*.

Worship is obedient service manifesting through self-sacrifice.

A Kingdom Witness
REDEMPTIVE COMPONENTS

Without having redemptive components available in what we read, watch, and generally participate in, people run the risk of forgetting what such components are and why they're important. The ability for followers of Christ to function as salt and light among the cultures of the world is therefore diminished. As a result, human beings will continually live and die in darkness without even realizing it. (Jn. 1:5, 8:12, 9:5, 12:36, and Eph. 5:8)

- Redemptive: Of, related to, or bringing about redemption
- Components: Something put together; a compound; an ingredient

A PSA
FOR THOSE OVER 40

Here's a PSA for anyone over 40 who cares to consider it: Everyone under 40 has no personal history with anything that's happened on the planet prior to their birth. Please be advised that your perspective on how life once worked is not shared by the vast number of them.

Thanks for your attention. I now return you to your current life situation…

A Pondering
TREE / ACORN

These are the branches from our family tree:
I am Richard Wayne Berry / The son of William Lee Berry / The son of Rufus Henry Berry / The son of John Lee Berry / The son of George Washington Berry / My son is Jesse Aaron Berry / The father of Benaiah Sibusiso Berry (my grandson, one year old today) / and *Caleb Mawandumusa Berry (grandson #2). That's a bunch of Berry boys right there.

I WILL NOT RUN

My great-grandfather was an angry man, he abused his family
He passed along that heritage, through the roots of our family tree
His children turned against him, and they drove him from his home
Never knowing where he ended up, or if he died alone

My grandfather was an honest man, he tried to live what's right
But somehow in darkness he fell without a fight
He took his sons, and his dignity, and he climbed into his truck
And he drove off in the shadows, trying to change his string of luck

I will not run, I will not run
By God's grace, I'll stand and face, each new day as it comes
I will not run, I will not run
The family curse has been reversed, the healing has begun
For I will not run...

My father was a godly man, of that there is no doubt
He told me once when he was young, he tried finding his way out
But, his love for God, and mom, and me, was stronger than his fear
So Jesus Christ was honored through the life dad lived down here

I will not run, I will not run
By God's grace I'll stand and face, each new day as it comes
I will not run, I will not run
The family curse has been reversed, now there's a blessing for my son
For I will not run...

(W. Berry / See & Say Songs, BMI)

ADDENDUM #1

In 2012, our son, Jesse Aaron, moved to Zimbabwe, Africa to serve on the mission field. While there, he met, courted, fell in love, and married Sista Lily in March of 2014. They returned to the U.S. in 2016 to establish themselves stateside, and begin a family. In August of 2017, their son Benaiah Sibusiso, was born. In Ndebele, his mother's native language, *Sibusiso* means *blessing*.

If you'll look at the last line of the song above you'll see the phrase, "now there's a blessing for my son." That line, and that song, were composed several years before Jesse had even given a thought to sojourning to the African continent. It is stunning, and humbling to see the ways in which God works His will in details both small and large.

ADDENDUM #2:

In January of this year, Jesse and Sista had their second son. Caleb Mawandumusa joined us just as the global pandemic was beginning to spread. His arrival has been a source of joy and inspiration as life on the planet has been radically turned upside down. In Ndebele, *Mawandumusa* means *may God's favor continue to increase.* His new life is an encouragement for us in the daze we're living in.

Personal Observations
ON WORSHIP LEADERSHIP

A person who leads songs in church is a song leader. A person who leads worship songs in church is a leader of worship songs.

A person who leads worship songs in church—having developed some personal understanding of what worship is and how it is to be practiced (i.e. worship theology)—is a worship leader. (See Rom. 12:1–2 MSG)

A person who carries worship in their head and heart (See Jn. 4:24)—with a desire to impart what they carry to both individuals and congregations—is a worship pastor. (See Deut. 10:8 and 2 Chron. 35:2-4)

Selah…pause and consider.

Counting Down
TICK-TOCK

One of the most challenging things about living a kingdom lifestyle is attempting to do so as clock time is going on around us externally, while maintaining eternal time internally. Why is that? Because eternal time has no beginning, middle, or end. It is—eternal. Earth time takes place within the framework structured (created) by God. It provides a context in which the unfolding of history happens while humankind inhabits the earth. The very first phrase in the Bible tells us that's the case: "In the beginning..." Scripture is not speaking about eternity, since eternity has no beginning. Therefore, what's being referred to are the boundaries of earth time—morning and evening, day one, etc.

> *"But as for me, I trust in You, O Lord, I say, "You are my God." My times are in Your hand..."*
>
> ~Ps. 31:14–15a

Ponder this: There are two kinds of time. One is temporal, earth-bound, having a beginning, middle, and end. The other is eternal, with no beginning, middle, or end. It was, is, and always will be. If the psalmist had said, "my time is in your hand," he would have limited his trust to life here on the planet. But, by saying, "my *time(s)* are in your hand," he was extending his trust in the Lord to include both constructs—here and there. It's astounding how Scripture does stuff like that. FYI: The word *times* in Strong's Concordance means *now, when, after, and always. Continually. From a word meaning in perpetuity; without end.*

A Biblical POV
THINGS ABOVE
(Col. 3:1-3)

In his book entitled, *The Unshakable Kingdom And The Unchanging Person*, E. Stanley Jones offers personal insight and revelation regarding life lived in God's eternal kingdom —the yesterday, today, and forever(ness) of it all. He provides an excerpt from an article written by Stewart Alsop and published in *Reader's Digest* in February of 1971. It says in part, "the fact is that the radically chic—or whatever you want to call it—is essentially a fad, and all fads die. They occupy the obsessive attention of the nation for a time. Then they become a bore, and they die, utterly, overnight."

Dear saints, bear such as that in mind whenever you find yourself caught up in the current buzz of the day. I'd suggest that you do three things in that regard:
- Read and apply Ps. 131 to your daily life
- Do the same with Phil. 4:4-9
- Ponder this passage on a regular basis:

"So here's what I want you to do, God helping you: Take your everyday, ordinary life—your sleeping, eating, going-to-work,

PARTICULAR PONDERING(S)

and walking-around life—and place it before God as an *offering. Embracing what God does for you is the best thing you can do for him. Don't become so well-adjusted to your culture that you fit into it without even thinking. Instead, fix your attention on God. You'll be changed from the inside out. Readily recognize what he wants from you, and quickly respond to it. Unlike the culture around you, always dragging you down to its level of immaturity, God brings the best out of you, develops well-formed maturity in you."

~Rom. 12:1–2 (MSG)

*Offering in the KJV is translated as "living sacrifice". The NASB says that such a sacrifice is our "reasonable service of worship".

Selah…pause and consider.

SET YOUR SIGHTS ABOVE

Set your affections on things above and not on earthly things
For you have died, and your life is hidden with Christ in God
So brothers be thankful and let His Word reign in your hearts with love
Serve one another, take care of each other
And set your sights above

If you are risen with Christ your Savior, then He is your all in all
And the peace of God living in your hearts is the peace to which you're called
So sisters be thankful and let His word reign in your hearts with love
Serve one another, as sisters and brothers, and set your sights above

Learn perfectness through charity

THINGS ABOVE

Doing all in Jesus' name
Giving praise to God with faithfulness
For the glory of His name

REPEAT FIRST VERSE:
                    (W. Berry / See & Say Songs, BMI)

A Pondering
A PHASES PHRASE

Retirement to Rebootment to Recalibration to Solitary Refinement. The process continues…
I supposed you could say I'm being phased out. That'd be ok. I'm all right with that.

"I go the way of all the earth."

~1 Kings 2:2 (KJV)

A Pondering
HUMILITY AND EXALTATION

> "Anything that leaves you at the center is off-center."
> ~E. Stanley Jones (See 1 Pet. 5:6.)

The central pattern of character in the Kingdom is that of a servant-minded ruler. (Mt. 20:25-28)
The central slogan in the kingdom of God is:

> *"Seek first the kingdom of God, and all these things (including yourself) will be added unto you."*
> ~Mt. 23:5-12 (MOF)

Whoever uplifts himself will be humbled, and whoever humbles himself will be uplifted. It's truly amazing to me how the Bible can speak to any and all generations. That is, if we'll pay attention.

Before you read the verse below, be advised that I'm aware that there is a context for it which may or may not apply today. However, my intention isn't to address our current national or global political situation. Neither am I intending to mess with anyone's personal theology. Nor am I trying to create some sort of new doctrinal approach to address global chaos. I'm merely pointing out the language in the text. What you do with it is your business.

> "You are not to say, 'It is a conspiracy!' In regard to all that this people call a conspiracy, and you are not to fear what they fear or be in dread of it. It is the Lord of hosts whom you should regard as holy. And He shall be your fear, and He shall be your dread."
>
> ~Isa. 8:12–13

Same text, different rendering.

> "Don't be like this people, always afraid somebody is plotting against them. Don't fear what they fear. Don't take on their worries. If you're going to worry, worry about The Holy. Fear God-of-the-Angel-Armies. The Holy can be either a Hiding Place or a Boulder blocking your way..."
>
> ~Isa. 8:12–13 (MSG)

Perhaps the following Scriptural input can help to gain a clearer Biblical perspective:

> "Be cheerful with joyous celebration in every season of life. Let joy overflow, for you are united with the Anointed One! Let gentleness be seen in every relationship, for our Lord is ever near.
>
> Don't be pulled in different directions or worried about a thing. Be saturated in prayer throughout each day, offering your faith-filled requests before God with overflowing gratitude. Tell him every detail of your life, then God's wonderful peace that transcends human understanding, will make the

answers known to you through Jesus Christ. So keep your thoughts continually fixed on all that is authentic and real, honorable and admirable, beautiful and respectful, pure and holy, merciful and kind. And fasten your thoughts on every glorious work of God, praising him always. Follow the example of all that we have imparted to you and the God of peace will be with you in all things."

~Phil. 4:4-9 (TPT)

"Humble yourselves, therefore, under the mighty hand of God so that at the proper time he may exalt you."

~1 Pet. 5:6 (ESV)

It's our job to humble ourselves. It's God's job to exalt us—in His time, on His terms. If we insist on doing His job, He has no option left but to do ours.

Selah…pause and consider.

A Pondering
SOJOURNERS UPDATE

In May of last year (2017), I retired from full time staff ministry. At that point, OUTBOUND MINISTRIES INTERNATIONAL became the framework from which Jean and I now serve the body of Christ worldwide. I was in what I called my reboot phase till March of this year when we embarked on our first official mission outreach back to the African continent.

During a month of service—teaching/preaching/leading seminars/and continued discipleship building—the Holy Ghost gave me a word regarding what was to happen next. It had to do with a spiritual life-shift that was to take place. The word was *recalibration*. We returned from that sojourn in April, and since then I've been pondering exactly what this current season of recalibration means—how it works, what my responsibility to it is, and just how long it may continue.

The pondering continues.

> *"Blessed are those whose strength is in You / Who've set their hearts on pilgrimage / As they pass through the valley of tears / They make it a place of springs / They go from strength to*

strength / Till each appears before God in Zion."

~Ps. 84:5-7

As of today, this is what I've determined to do in that regard:

Yield to the Spirit requesting that He take me to a new level of intercessory service on behalf of others (see Phil. 4:4-9 / Heb.4:16).

Continue to unpack and study 2 Cor. 5:18-21 which I consider to be a timely and critically relevant passage as it relates to two key areas in the life of every follower of Christ:
- Offering the "ministry of reconciliation" (which is the job description of every Christian)
- Learn what it means to serve as an "ambassador of Christ" (which is the job title of every Christian)

Focus in on what it means to live a kingdom lifestyle, and how to share that with others as a "teaching Levite" (see 2 Chron. 35:2-4).

Remain open to and teachable regarding how to better love and serve my wife of 38 years.

Establish deeper relationships with my grown children as their adult lives develop.

Revel in grandparenting our grandsons.

A Biblical POV
LIGHT VS. DARKNESS

"Where you gonna go for some illumination?"
                                            ~B. Cockburn

"... for you were formerly darkness, but now you are Light in the Lord; walk as children of Light (for the fruit of the Light consists in all goodness and righteousness and truth), trying to learn what is pleasing to the Lord. Do not participate in the unfruitful deeds of darkness, but instead even expose them; for it is disgraceful even to speak of the things which are done by them in secret."
                                            ~Eph. 5:8-12

Notice (if you haven't already) that every single grouping mentioned in the verse below is past tense. That means if you are a follower of Christ, you are already included in each category. You just need to live like you know that.

"But [you] are God's [chosen treasure]—[priests] who are [kings], a [spiritual nation] [set apart as God's devoted ones]. He called you [out of darkness to experience his marvelous

light], and now [he claims you as his very own]. He did this so that you would broadcast his glorious wonders throughout the world."

~1 Pet. 2:9 (TPT, emphasis mine)

"It's better to light a candle than to curse the darkness."
~Chinese proverb

I've been scraping little shavings off my ration of light
and I've formed it into a ball
And each time I pack a bit more onto it
and I make a bowl of my hands
And I scoop it from its secret cache under a loose board in the floor
And I blow across it and I send it to you
Against those moments when the darkness blows under your door
Isn't that what friends are for?

Isn't that What Friends are For, Bruce Cockburn
© Rotten Kiddies Music Llc, Bro N Sis Music, Inc
used by permission

There are three portions of Scripture which have impacted me deeply over the last several years.

"Is there any place I can go to avoid your Spirit to be out of your sight? If I climb to the sky, you're there! If I go underground, you're there! If I flew on morning's wings to the far western horizon, You'd find me in a minute—you're already there waiting! Then I said to myself, 'Oh, he even sees me in the dark! At night I'm immersed in the light!' It's a fact:

PARTICULAR PONDERING(S)

darkness isn't dark to you; night and day, darkness and light, they're all the same to you."

~Ps. 139:7-12 (MSG)

"I will give you the treasures of darkness and hidden wealth of secret places, So that you may know that it is I, the Lord, the God of Israel, who calls you by your name."

~Isa. 45:3

"Every gift God freely gives us is good and perfect, streaming down from the Father of lights, who shines from the heavens with no hidden shadow or darkness and is never subject to change."

~Ja. 1:17 (TPT)

Here's my take on each of those passages:

Ps. 139:7-12 is primarily showing us a Biblical perspective on God's omnipresence. That in itself deserves a considerable amount of attention. But here presently I'll only focus in on how verse 12 addresses light vs. darkness regarding one specific reality concerning the Father of lights.

Verse 12 says that darkness and light are the same to God. It states very clearly that there is no distinction between the two. That is a mind-blowing statement to ponder. The implications are profound in relationship to how we view our Sovereign Creator and how He Himself views darkness.

If darkness and light are in fact the same to God, then from His perspective there is no difference between the two. In other words, from God's vantage point there is no such thing as darkness being separate from light. Why? How can that be? Because according to the text, they are the same to Him. I cannot explain how that is with any fitting degree of clarity. However, I can—by faith—take the Word to mean exactly what it says—which I do.

The Isaiah 45 text calls for a little more contextual consideration in order to see its linkage with the Ps. 139 passage:

To begin with, the prophet Isaiah is addressing someone in specific, not others in general. However, those who have been "churched"—trained by Scripture—are aware that the appropriation of the Bible into their own lives can be, and very often should be, understood and accepted as being available and intended for public as well as personal application. That being said, the fact that chapter 45 is directed toward Cyrus doesn't exclude other followers of Christ from relating to it—at least on some level. Stated simply, what the prophet passed along to Cyrus can be applied to our lives if we'll allow the Holy Ghost to help us appropriate it personally and corporately.

Look again at verse 3 which states, *"I will give you treasures of darkness and hidden wealth of secret places, so that you may know that it is I, the Lord, the God of Israel, who calls you by your name."*

Notice the following:
- There are treasures hidden in darkness
- The Lord knows where they are and what they are
- The places themselves are secret along with the treasures hidden there
- The reason that the treasures and the places are to be revealed is so that those who are shown them will know that God Himself has called them to such places by His own doing

The incentive for causing us to re-examine how we understand darkness contained in those four points is huge. There is much more there than meets the eye so to speak. May the Holy Ghost help us to refocus our attention on what the Word is trying to convey to us about such matters. The process of doing that is known as systematic theology.

Systematic theology is a discipline of Christian theology that formulates an orderly, rational, and coherent account of the doctrines of the Christian faith. It addresses issues such as what the Bible teaches about certain topics or what is true about God and his universe. It also builds on biblical disciplines, church history, as well as biblical and historical theology. Systematic theology shares its systematic tasks with other disciplines such as constructive theology, dogmatics, ethics, apologetics, and philosophy of religion.

Those two passages are both found in an active state in the Old Testament. An echo—or extended vista—is also made available to us in the New Testament.

In James 1:17 we're told that there is *"no shadow of turning in Him."* The NASB translates that concept as *"no variation or shifting shadow."* In order for a shadow to be cast, there must first be a contrast between light and darkness which enables shadows to manifest. Without such a contrast it is impossible for a shadow to be formed let along made visible. Therefore, if darkness and light are the same to God and if He is present everywhere (Omnipresent / Ps. 139:7-12), then everywhere He is there is no contrast or distinction present in such an atmosphere that is fully charged with holy brightness.

Note as well that the James text says that *"every good and perfect gift"* is made available by God. Recall that the Isaiah text mentioned above says that there are *"treasures of darkness"* hidden in *"secret places"* which are available to those whom God chooses to reveal and impart them to. Perhaps you'll want to pause here to consider the implications of what I'm saying—based on my understanding of the three specific passages.

I've said all that in order to get to here:

We have been taught (predisposed) to do all we can to avoid darkness. Reject it. Run from it. Distance ourselves from it in any way we can. There are many Scriptures which reinforce such a viewpoint regarding darkness. So, theologically speaking that is not an incorrect practice to follow. However, there is another viewpoint which is altogether different—or other—from that mentioned, or implied, in the Isa. 45:3 text.

If there are hidden treasures in secret places which God says He will share with those who for whatever reason find themselves there, why is running away from such places our only course of appropriate action?

Just suppose that such dark places—filled with hidden treasures—are made available to those who are willing to claim them in order to bring them out and make them available to others for their benefit.

Note that I am not suggesting that anyone ever purposely venture into such dark places on their own in order to acquire such treasures. That'd be stupid and scripturally inappropriate. What I'm saying is this: If/When we find ourselves in dark places we should bear this in mind:

Where God is present darkness doesn't exist for there is *"no shadow of turning in Him."* The places may *appear* to be dark, but they aren't if He is present. And since He's omnipresent, darkness cannot *really* be where He is. Are you seeing a pattern here?

If, for whatever reason, God has chosen to show us a dark place we should remember that's where hidden treasures are. Perhaps He's placed us in such circumstances in order to pass along things that aren't available anywhere else.

PARTICULAR PONDERING(S)

The entire process I've just laid out is said to be taking place so that we'll know He's called us into and out of such conditions. (See again Ja. 1:17.)

Here's a word of wisdom intended to wise us up:

"My fellow believers, when it seems as though you are facing nothing but difficulties see it as an invaluable opportunity to experience the greatest joy that you can! For you know that when your faith is tested it stirs up power within you to endure all things. And then as your endurance grows even stronger it will release perfection into every part of your being until there is nothing missing and nothing lacking."

~Ja. 1:2 (TPT)

A Reminder
PONDERING GRACE

Grace is the unmerited favor of God's empowering presence, enabling me to be who He created me to be, so I can do what He calls me to do.

Grace in/on our lives can be perceived (known) through observation) by others:

> "...*recognizing (perceiving) the grace that had been given to me...*"
>
> ~Gal. 2:9

A Biblical POV
THEOLOGICAL ADJUSTMENTS

There are far too many Christians today who think Rom. 8:28 reads as follows:

"And we know that God causes all (good) things to work for good to those who love God, to those who are called according to His purpose."

Please be advised that the word *good* is not really in the text. Inserting it there will cause a considerable amount of personal problems when trying to walk out a life of faith.

Selah…pause and consider.

A Biblical POV
SOVEREIGNTY

There's no such thing as being partially sovereign. A person is sovereign or they're not. I should add that goes for a place (or nation) as well. To unpack that a little more…

A component of a sovereign life is that one is, or should be, considered as being in charge of anyone, anything, and everything under their rule. Any persons under such a charge who are not yielded, or will not yield to sovereign leadership would be considered as being insubordinate, rebellious, or disloyal. Bear in mind that there are serious repercussions for living in such a state of disobedience. The results of trying to live out from under a sovereign ruler can be costly—in some cases even deadly. So, the matter of who's in charge of your life—you, or a Sovereign—should be considered of major importance here on the planet, and over into eternity as well.

Having said that, let's revisit a Bible verse which deals, by implication, with God's position over His creation—according to His will, His Word, and His way(s).

"And we know that for those who love God all things work

together for good, for those who are called according to his purpose."

~Rom.8:28 (ESV)

Here's an alternate rendering of Rom.8:28.

"If He who can doesn't, then it must be better so."

~Dr. M. Smith

Over the last decade or so, I've begun to notice what seems to be a misappropriation of what that verse clearly states. Some—way too many—are now inserting a word which isn't there. The word is *good*, and here's how it is injected into the text:

"And we know that for those who love God all good *things work together for good…"*

Such a reinterpretation shows a gross misunderstanding of the principle and place of the sovereignty of God. To do so creates, and in turn imparts, a theology that stinks! It smells to high heaven because it's rotten. A professor of mine in daze past called such a mind-set "stinkin' thinkin'." That term seems in order here.

Entitlement has found its way into the body of Christ at-large in profound and damaging ways. On a base level, it allows so-called followers of Christ to move out from under God's Divine authority as it suits them—founded on their personal entitlement as King's Kids. All that has to do with how destiny is viewed. But that's another story for another time.

When we view theology from a slant toward entitlement we dumb down the cause and effect principle of the Word, making it silly and simple-minded. As that takes place we begin to view the unfolding of our lives as born again believers as being either blessed of the Lord, or cursed by the devil. I could say so much more about this entire process, but there's really no need to do that. Just read the entire book of Job—slowly and prayerfully. It speaks to what I'm addressing here much better than I ever could.

One last comment: If we consider ourselves followers of Christ, then we have to find a way to process this verse.

"Yet though He slay me, still will I trust Him."
-Job 13:15

*"Jesus did not come to explain away suffering or remove it.
He came to fill it with His presence."*
-Paul Claudel

A Pondering
PROCESSING "THE PRESENCE"

CORRIDOR OF LIGHT
(Isa.2 :2-5)

If I'm in a bad circumstance, with very few choices
Caught up in the chaos, and hearing strange voices
There's a path that I can take, it's the way for me to go
Down the corridor of light, there's a hand that I can hold

CHORUS:
When I'm liftin' up Jesus, when I'm liftin' up Jesus
When I'm liftin' up Jesus, I'm takin' demons down

Even at the end of the age, there's a promise I can claim
I can dignify my trials, when I call upon His name
Then in the middle of the warfare, or at the end of my rope
I'll see the corridor of light, where there's a glimmer left of hope

REPEAT CHORUS:

(We're movin') from glory to glory, from strength to strength
From one level to another, we're all done with unbelief

PROCESSING "THE PRESENCE"

With our eyes toward Zion, God's "holy hill"
We'll see the corridor of light, that shines and always will

REPEAT CHORUS:
(W. Berry / See & Say Songs, BMI)

I've found what I believe is a Biblically-based process for how God's manifest presence can be seen, tracked, and understood from scripture. Others have most certainly seen it as well. Some have done a much better job than I'm about to attempt by trying to explain it. Here's the process in its simplest form:

From Presence to Power to Position to Proclamation
(Ex. 33:13-17, Acts 1:8, 2 Cor. 5:18-21, Heb. 2:10)

To unpack it I'll begin in The Garden just after The Fall. I've just mention that this could take a while to present. So, here goes...

Since God is omnipresent, He is everywhere all the time. In other words, there is no place where God isn't. But the theology of omnipresence wasn't available when Adam and Eve were the only ones around to receive and relate to it. There was no need for that theology to be in place as such since they had an unbroken intimate relationship with their Creator. Theology had to evolve over time, and the evolution started in Genesis chapter 3, verse 8.

> *"And they heard the sound of the Lord God walking in the garden in the cool] of the day, and the man and his wife hid themselves from the presence of the Lord God among the trees of the garden."*
>
> —Gen. 3:8 (ESV)

PARTICULAR PONDERING(S)

Note the phrase *"hid themselves from the presence."* That statement makes it clear that an understanding/comprehension of omnipresence didn't exist in that place and time. It's impossible to hide from someone who is everywhere all the time. That's what omnipresence means. And that's what God is.

Adam and Eve thought that Jehovah was only around when they were aware of Him through some type of manifested experience—walking in the garden in the cool of the day for example. In other words, without some type of sign—physical evidence—they seemed to think He wasn't anywhere to be found. Why do I say that? Because why else would they have decided that they should hide themselves when they heard Him coming if they had been aware that He was there already present—everywhere, all the time?

The conviction—shame—they experienced after their disobedience only took place when they were *aware* that He had apparently returned to join them there in The Garden. Such awareness was based on having an experience. Their error in judgment—their lack of spiritual discernment and maturity—was entirely based on having no theology for omnipresence. Which I must add is still a problem in the lives of a great many followers of Christ even today. Evidence isn't intended to replace faith in our spiritual walk. Evidence is certainly of some value. But it is not a replacement for faith. It is to be the manifestation of faith itself.

> *"Faith is the substance of things hoped for, the evidence of things not seen."*
>
> ~Heb.11:1

That verse states clearly that the specific kind of evidence that followers of Christ are to live by is that of faith. Walking by faith, not by sight, means exactly what it says. (2 Cor. 5:7)

When there is no apparent evidence of God's presence the result is that many born again believers think He's simply not around. Jonah had that problem too—but that's another story altogether. Such a perspective as that is as biblically inaccurate today as it was then. Ps. 139:7-12 makes that clear, as does 1 Cor. 3:16. But, I'm getting ahead of myself. There's a considerable distance to cover between Genesis 3 and Ps. 139 and on to 1 Cor. 3:16. So I'd best backtrack in order to follow the pathway process I opened this narrative with.

REPEATING
From Presence to Power to Position to Proclamation
(Ex. 33:13-17, Acts 1:8, 2 Cor. 5:18-21, Heb.2:10)

I'm fairly certain that Scripture offers us many examples of the lack of a theology of presence following after the scene we've just looked at. But, I haven't researched them enough to include them here. However, I do know that there was a lack of understanding in that regard still taking place all the way up to and including what transpired in Exodus, chapter 33. There we encounter one of the most important stories in the Bible, along with (from my perspective) perhaps the most important prayer regarding the living and active presence of God in the lives of His people—His indwelling. The movement from the external to the internal is still being actively outworked today. That transference, that outworking, is the next stop along the pathway of processing presence.

"Moses said to the Lord, "See, you say to me, 'Bring up this

PARTICULAR PONDERING(S)

> *people,' but you have not let me know whom you will send with me. Yet you have said, 'I know you by name, and you have also found favor in my sight.' Now therefore, if I have found favor in your sight, please show me now your ways, that I may know you in order to find favor in your sight. Consider too that this nation is your people.*
>
> *"And he said, "My presence will go with you, and I will give you rest."*
>
> *"And he said to him, "If your presence will not go with me, do not bring us up from here. For how shall it be known that I have found favor in your sight, I and your people? Is it not in your going with us, so that we are distinct, I and your people, from every other people on the face of the earth?""*
>
> ~Ex. 33:12-16 (ESV)

If you choose to, you can sort out the proper context for the scene presented above in that text. In fact, that'd likely be a good idea. I'm only looking at the specifics taking place between Moses and Jehovah which prompted the prayer he offered up.

To begin with, the entire prayer is based on the need for Presence as Moses understood it. Based on that objective here are the dynamics involved:

Moses' request to know Jehovah's ways is first on behalf of himself and the direct link to the people he's leading. In other words, the prayer is not self-serving. Rather, it is representative of his desire for clearly defined direction in order to follow the Presence in obedience. His concern is for everyone who has been living and sojourning under the cloud to remain covered so to speak. Up to this point, the cloud and the pillar of fire have been the manifestations they needed in order to rest assured that Jehovah was, in fact, with them. As I see it, that's an exact duplication of what Adam and Eve had done by needing physical evidence in order to believe. There's no faith in that approach to embracing Presence.

Moses does not ask for blessings, material goods, healings, deliverance, etc. His prayer for *all* the needs he and those he's leading require is one thing and only one thing: *Presence*!

God gives Moses the answer he's prayerfully requested. In turn Moses reveals the bottom line intention of his plea.

> *"If your presence will not go with me, do not bring us up from here. For how shall it be known that I have found favor in your sight, I and your people? Is it not in your going with us, so that we are distinct, I and your people, from every other people on the face of the earth?"*

His prayer is that the collective/corporate witness of God's people would manifest as their testimony to any and all others they'd come in contact with in their ongoing sojourn. The implication is that the very presence of God among them would serve as all that's necessary for them to represent their God to those who didn't know Him. According to how the prayer is worded, no other signs and wonders were considered necessary. No other miracles of any kind—just Presence in their midst. The language in the Hebrew gets even more specific regarding the reason for such a request.

The word *distinct* (separated in the KJV) means, distinguished; put as different; shown to be marvelous, set apart, made wonderful. *Wow!* Talk about a dynamic witness. What an impactive and impressive way to show forth (live out) a living testimony—just carry this *Presence!* (See 1 Pet. 2:9.)

Thereafter God's answer to Moses' prayer is clearly and certainly affirmed through the Biblical stories which follow in Scripture. Throughout those events, the theology of omnipresence continues to evolve in ways far too numerous to delve into here. They all lead, as I've tracked them, to what the Psalmist declares:

> *"Is there any place I can go to avoid your Spirit to be out of your sight? If I climb to the sky, you're there! If I go underground, you're there! If I flew on morning's wings to the far western horizon, You'd find me in a minute — you're already there waiting! Then I said to myself, 'Oh, he even sees me in the dark! At night I'm immersed in the light!' It's a fact: darkness isn't dark to you; night and day, darkness and light, they're all the same to you."*
>
> ~Ps. 139:7-12 (MSG)

From the reading of that text I have no doubt that omnipresence has found its place in the process. David's words could not be any clearer than they are there. Nor can there be any question that Moses' prayer way back in Ex. 33 had been answered exactly as Jehovah stated that it would. The fact that Jehovah responded to Moses in the affirmative is in fact still being fulfilled today. In that sense, Moses' supplication for God's abiding and sustaining presence to "go with" His people continues to unfold in the lives of followers of Christ as I'm writing this sentence. Astounding! Almost unbelievable! Overwhelming! Truly *awesome*!

The entire process that I've just laid out—based on Scripture—has been leading from presence to power. That's where the pathway has brought us to now. And, here's what happens next. Continuing the journey, look at (revisit) Acts 1:8 (KJV).

"But ye shall receive power, after that the Holy Ghost is come upon you: and ye shall be witnesses unto me both in Jerusalem, and in all Judaea, and in Samaria, and unto the uttermost part of the earth."

The text says something that the contemporary church seems to have overlooked in the last couple of generations. The phrase *"after that the Holy Ghost is come"* is an event which took place —and still takes place—once the Presence of God has come first. In other words, the power to *be* witnesses was/is proceeded by the indwelling presence of the Lord. No Presence, no power. No power, no purpose (witness). No witness, no testimony. No testimony, no proclamation, no proclamation, no conversion, revival, restoration, or renewal.

Without spiritual empowerment, the advancement and expansion of the Kingdom of God is limited/restricted/impeded—slowed way down in terms of advancing momentum, growth and influence. That is to say that the charge given to the followers of Christ spoken by Jesus, "on earth as it is in heaven," is a much harder task to accomplish than it has to be. Such a lack of power has set in place an organized-church-based-structure which produces a gospel with little to no real relevance in regards to the very people who Moses prayed would be impacted by God's presence going with them—those who don't know Him as King of kings, and Lord of lords. Right about here is where your tears should start to fall. Mine are.

The mandate given to the disciples by Jesus is the so-called Great Commission (Mt. 28:18-20). It was to be energized by the active Presence of God, which in turn released the power of the Holy Ghost; transforming the disciples into witnesses; which prompted their testimony; ultimately enabling worldwide proclamation, conviction, conversion, and Kingdom expansion (i.e. revival). God's response to Moses' prayer began that process. Its fulfilment is still at work today.

When presence is not properly understood (from a perspective of Omnipresence), then any number of things can be substituted as being of major (or more) importance. When the church allows its focus to be on other things, we can lose the awareness of His active presence. If that goes unchecked, we then, over time, begin to do *Christian stuff* in our own strength. Forgetting that Presence precedes power can mess up our lives, our congregations, our witness, and our testimony (proclamation) big time.

Sadly, I see that as the current state of much of the body of Christ.

This pathway of processing Presence leads from here on to our personal responsibility in and for God's kingdom presented in 2 Cor. 5:18-21. There we are presented two key components directly related to our lives lived out "in Christ" (See Col. 3:1-3). Those components are our job description and our job title.

God Almighty, El 'Elyon, the Most High God (Ps. 104) has a Divine purpose in mind for releasing an awareness of His Presence to humanity. That's such an immense subject to ponder, the depth and breadth of which requires much more insight, knowledge, understanding, and wisdom than I have. I will however continue considering how such a purpose is outworked in relation to the very Presence of God being available, and at work both in earth time and in eternity.

An Axiom
Knowledge is Information
Understanding is Interpretation
Wisdom is Application

NO OTHER GOD

No other God can claim the place You hold in my heart
No other God can break the bond You hold to my heart
All the praise I have, I offer up to You

CHORUS:
In worship of the Most High God
In worship of the Most High God
In worship of the Most High God

No other God can speak the words of life to my soul
No other God can sweep away the night's dark glow
REPEART CHORUS:

You are Holy, and worthy to be praised
You are righteous, and just in all Your ways
You are faithful, compassionate and true
God Almighty, I give myself to You

REPEAT CHORUS:

(W. Berry / See & Say Songs, BMI)

I'm including three different translations of 2 Cor. 5:18-21 in order to provide a broader perspective of what it says. Please consider them carefully.

PARTICULAR PONDERING(S)

"Now all these things are from God, who reconciled us to Himself through Christ and gave us the ministry of reconciliation, namely, that God was in Christ reconciling the world to Himself, not counting their trespasses against them, and He has committed to us the word of reconciliation. Therefore, we are ambassadors for Christ, as though God were making an appeal through us; we beg you on behalf of Christ, be reconciled to God. He made Him who knew no sin to be sin on our behalf, so that we might become the righteousness of God in Him."

~2 Cor. 5:18-21

"And God has made all things new, and reconciled us to himself, and given us the ministry of reconciling others to God. In other words, it was through the Anointed One that God was shepherding the world, not even keeping records of their transgressions, and he has entrusted to us the ministry of opening the door of reconciliation to God. We are ambassadors of the Anointed One who carry the message of Christ to the world, as though God were tenderly pleading with them directly through our lips. So we tenderly plead with you on Christ's behalf, 'Turn back to God and be reconciled to him.' For God made the only one who did not know sin to become sin for us, so that we who did not know righteousness might become the righteousness of God through our union with him."

~2 Cor. 5:18-21 (TPT)

"Because of this decision we don't evaluate people by what they have or how they look. We looked at the Messiah that way once and got it all wrong, as you know. We certainly

don't look at him that way anymore. Now we look inside, and what we see is that anyone united with the Messiah gets a fresh start, is created new. The old life is gone; a new life burgeons! Look at it! All this comes from the God who settled the relationship between us and him, and then called us to settle our relationships with each other. God put the world square with himself through the Messiah, giving the world a fresh start by offering forgiveness of sins. God has given us the task of telling everyone what he is doing. We're Christ's representatives. God uses us to persuade men and women to drop their differences and enter into God's work of making things right between them. We're speaking for Christ himself now: Become friends with God; he's already a friend with you. How? you ask. In Christ. God put the wrong on him who never did anything wrong, so we could be put right with God."
~2 Cor. 5:18-21 (MSG)

That passage reveals a great deal of God's purpose for presence becoming resident and available to humankind. This is how I see it as revealed in the text:

God was in Christ in order to provide those who are, through redemption, "in Christ" (Col. 3:3) with the ministry of reconciliation. If the ministry of reconciliation was given to Christ, then those who are living their lives in Him share in the exact same ministry as His. And, since those who are redeemed are already reconciled, such a ministry must be by its very nature intended for those who are not yet reconciled—the unredeemed. What I mean to say is that such a ministry of reconciliation can only be offered and extended by those who are saved/reconciled to those who aren't. Don't let that slip by you, it's an important aspect of what's to follow.

PARTICULAR PONDERING(S)

The text continues by saying that, *"God was in Christ reconciling the world to Himself."* That being the case, I'm prompted to put this question before you. When did that happen? In other words, when did God do that? I believe the answer has to do with how we understand time and eternity. I'll try to explain what I mean by that.

NOTE: This'll likely be were some of the confusion I mentioned at the beginning of this narrative might appear. So, take it slow as you're reading. You've probably not given much thought (if any) to the following concept.

Eternity is timeless. That's why it's called eternity. It has no beginning, middle, or end. It was, is, and will be. The very first line in the Bible tells us where time itself comes from: *"In the beginning God..."* In the beginning of what? Since eternity has no consideration or measurement of time, and the Father, Son, and Holy Ghost all exist—three in one—in eternity, then they were not, are not, and will not be bound by it. So, when Scripture tells us that God did something "in the beginning" it is conveying the idea that the something being done (or created) was taking place in eternity—outside of (prior to) time. After its conception it was then introduced into the earth as an earth-bound distinctive. That was its beginning. In other words, time was created by God in eternity, and then inserted into/on to earth as a restrictive or limiting measurement (i.e. "evening and morning, one day" / Gen. 1:5). A framework if you will. Most of us miss that important detail by mentally skipping directly to the Creation Story without first considering the information which took place prior to the unfolding of creation itself. To try and clarify: The Creation Story took place *after* God first created time and then placed all of the history of earth and humankind within the context (framework) of what can best be called "earth-time." This all relates to the 2 Cor. 5 passage we're considering. Stay focused on that please. It'll all link together as you continue following my narrative.

I believe that the answer to the question I posed as to when was God in Christ reconciling the world to Himself is—before time began. That transaction took place before Jesus ever showed up on earth. In fact, it took place before anyone showed up, before time began, in eternity. That in turn prompts another question: Why is that important?

It's important because in order for *all* of the sin(s) of *all* humanity to be considered as *"not counting their trespasses against them,"* an event had to be in place which would cover *all* humanity prior to any acts of unrighteousness having taken place. Otherwise there would have been no way for God to have activated/contained reconciliation in Jesus. Why? Because an untold number of humans had lived, and sinned, on earth before Christ ever took on bodily form. Having placed the "fullness of the Godhead bodily in Christ (Col. 2:9), the Father was able to make the ministry of reconciliation available in His Son retro-actively, from before time began and through to the Second Coming, the end of the age, and then on into eternity, which is where it was conceived and manifested before earth was formed, *"before the foundation of the earth"* (Eph. 1:4).

What I've just stated may bring to your mind the question of how reconciliation took place prior to Christ becoming our Messiah. To answer that you'll have to consult with someone other than me. I'm not qualified or prepared to attempt an answer at this time or in this fashion.

Is your head hurting? Take a break and come back to this later. I'm not finished.

Our text under consideration then states that God has

PARTICULAR PONDERING(S)

"committed to us the word of reconciliation." (NASB). So, let's look at the word itself.

Reconciliation in Strong's Concordance means: To exchange or adjust; restoration to Divine favor; atonement. It comes from a root word meaning to change mutually; to compound (or unify) different.

Reconciliation has to do with taking two or more things which are different, disconnected, or disunified, and making them into a compounded (joined, connected) substance.

Our text said that God placed the fullness of that specific type of reconciliation directly into Christ Jesus. And that He did so by "not counting their (humankind's) trespasses against them." In other words, He made a way for the sin(s) of each and every individual to have their fallen nature—their sinfulness—not be positioned as a blockage between them and their Creator. And, He did so by making Christ the means of reconciliation to any and all who would receive Him as the Reconciler. The text goes on to say that He gave that specific ministry to us. The same ministry that He placed in Christ belongs to all those who are themselves in Christ. That being the case, here's something that every believer must come to terms with in the real world that we really live in. Are we capable of extending the very same ministry of reconciliation to *all* people by "not counting their trespasses against them?" As representatives of the Kingdom of God here "on earth as it is in heaven" the body of Christ at large and every child of God in specific must come to terms with what that means and how it is to be lived out.

Our text then tells us how we are to live out the reconciliation ministry we've been given. It says we are to serve as "ambassadors for Christ." To be clear here: Discharging our "ministry of reconciliation" is our job description. Doing so as "ambassadors for Christ" is our job title.

In order to function as an ambassador, there is more required than just stating the phrase verbally from memory. Repeating it doesn't mean we understand it, or apply it to our lives directly. To serve in such a capacity makes knowing something about what an ambassador is and how their duties are to be done a serious consideration. Here's some data that'll help to accomplish just that.

Here are two articles that share some solid data as to the role of an ambassador.1

How Can A Christian Be An Ambassador For Christ?

In his passage on reconciliation in 2 Cor. 5, Paul says that Christians are ambassadors for Christ (2 Cor. 5:20). An ambassador is an official envoy who represents a foreign sovereign, providing a link between his host country and the country he represents. Ambassadors work to build relations and develop policies that favor both the host and the home of the ambassador. An ambassador is appointed by the leadership of those he represents and is given authority to speak on their behalf.

An ambassador must walk a very fine line. He lives in one country, but he is responsible to another. He must represent the message of a leader who is not directly present. He must also embody the character of his home country, following laws and customs that are not necessarily known or even welcome in the host nation. He must do this all while respecting the laws and customs of that host.

In 2 Cor. 5, instead of a nation, Paul is an ambassador of the kingdom of God. Unlike modern political ambassadors, Paul did not originate from the "nation" he represented. He had to be adopted in, through Christ's sacrifice, and then he had to undergo a change of perspective. He was no longer a citizen of the world and he no longer saw things as a citizen of the world. He saw things through the perspective of a citizen of the kingdom of God — he was a new creation (2 Cor. 5:17).

Paul's work as ambassador was to spread his Ruler's message to his host nation. That message was reconciliation. God wanted to be personally reconciled to the people Paul lived with. In a way, Paul was asking his hosts to commit treason against the kingdom of the world and pledge citizenship to the kingdom of God.

They could then follow in Paul's footsteps by becoming an ambassador for Christ in their own lives—as can we. It starts with a change in citizenship. If we are to represent Jesus to the world, we must first belong to the kingdom of God instead of the kingdom of self. We must live by the standards of our new King, even though we are temporarily away from Him (2 Cor. 5:6-9). Most importantly, we must accept that this earth is not our home—our home awaits us, "eternal in the heavens" (2 Cor. 5:1)—even if we are imprisoned and abused by our host country (Eph. 6:20). Finally, ambassadors must then spread His message: that everyone is welcome to have such a relationship with God.

Being an ambassador for Christ is the fulfillment of the incredibly important kingdom perspective. To follow Christ means to give up the kingdom of self and the kingdom of the world, and pledge allegiance to the kingdom of God. It means our home is heaven, not earth. Our

responsibility is to tell others about that good news so they can join the kingdom of God as well.
https://www.compellingtruth.org/ambassador-for-Christ.htm

See also: https://www.cgg.org//index.cfm/fuseaction/Library.sr/CT/ARTB/k/871/How-Conduct-Ourselves-as-Ambassadors-for-Christ.htm

One of the very best books which inter-faces with the topic of ambassadorship is *The Most Important Person On Earth* by Myles Munroe. It is available at Amazon.com in book form. There is also a workbook for class study available as a resource. It is online in a PDF and there are some videos as well on YouTube.

TO REVIEW:

Presence releases the Power to proceed / Power establishes Witness / Witness offers Testimony (through physical and/or verbal response) / Testimony produces and fulfills Kingdom Expansion (Revival).

CLOSER TO THE CLOUD

If Your Spirit doesn't go before me, I'm not moving, I'm saying here
If Your fire doesn't light my path, then this is where I'll be
Until I know You've made a way, I'll keep resting, and waiting Lord
And listening till I hear You say, child, it's time

CHORUS:
Draw me closer to the cloud when it starts moving
Closer to the heart of what You're doing
Closer to the Kingdom I'm pursuing
Draw me closer to the cloud

PARTICULAR PONDERING(S)

If the glory of Your holy hand isn't on me, then I'm undone
How else can I fulfill Your plan, without Your blessed touch
No one else would understand, it's Your presence that changes me
So Father, this is where I'll stand until it's time

REPEAT CHORUS:
(W. Berry / See & Say Songs, BMI)

I've covered the process toward Presence as best I understand it moving from Presence (Ex. 33:13-16) to Power, Witness and Testimony (Acts 1:8, Mt. 28:18-20) and on to Purpose and Practice (2 Cor. 5:18-21). But I've not taken you to the final destination. There is one verse in particular which I believe holds the key which unlocks the gate which leads across the bridge spanning from The Garden all the way to The Second Coming and beyond. As best I can recall, I've never read a commentary about it, seen a video teaching, heard a sermon, or read an article which addressed it in any meaningful manner. It's located in Heb. 2:10 and it says this:

NOTE: Again I've used three translations in order to provide a clearer perspective.

"It makes good sense that the God who got everything started and keeps everything going now completes the work by making the Salvation Pioneer perfect through suffering as he leads all these people to glory."

~Heb. 2:10-13 (MSG)

Christ became man, not angel, to save mankind.
"What we actually see is Jesus, after being made temporarily inferior to the angels (and so subject to pain and death), in order that he should, in God's grace, taste death for every man,

now crowned with glory and honor. It was right and proper that in bringing many sons to glory, God (from whom and by whom everything exists) should make the leader of their salvation a perfect leader through the fact that he suffered. For the one who makes men holy and the men who are made holy share a common humanity. So that he is not ashamed to call them his brothers..."

~Heb. 2:10-12 (Phillips)

"For it was fitting that he, for whom and by whom all things exist, in bringing many sons to glory, should make the founder of their salvation perfect through suffering."

~Heb. 2:10 (ESV)

I'll start unpacking that verse by providing the definition of the word *perfect*. Strong's Concordance says: accomplished; completed; consummated (in character); consecrated, finished, fulfilled.

That is to say that Christ's work as the Savior of all humankind was finished on the Cross. Calvary was the exclamation point at the end of His sentence so to speak. What Jesus was sent to earth to accomplish was completed (perfected) at the crucifixion. In point of fact, Jesus Himself stated that His work here was done when He uttered, *"It is finished"* (Jn. 19:28-30). The finished work of salvation was accomplished through the suffering that our Lord endured for the redemption of humanity.

The verse I'm focused in on here tells us why in specific that took place. It says, *"in bringing many sons to glory."* The Father's will, carried out to completion through His Son, was set in motion—from inception to fulfillment—in order to populate heaven with Kingdom citizens. (See 1 Pet. 2:9). You may also want to re-read from Moses' prayer, verse 16 of Ex. 33 for a broader perspective.

Said another way, Christ Jesus became the doorway through which the entrance into eternal life could take place. He's not the key that unlocks it. He's the doorway Himself. His entire life from birth to death, burial, resurrection, and ascension took place in order to provide a way for those who receive Him as their Redeemer to transition from life here to life (with the Father, Son, and Holy Ghost) into eternity and eternally. (See Acts 26:18 and Col. 1:13.)

What's contained in this one verse as I've already stated, builds a bridge over time and history. If you were to walk out along it, you'd begin to see a vista that expands into a vision far beyond what human eyes can see. The view from there provides a supernatural glimpse from here to eternity. An unveiling of what's been transpiring on earth throughout earth-time all the way into everlasting glory.

The Divine design regarding the relationship between the Creator and His creation was for ongoing and abiding presence to be inner-active and unbroken. An intimate bonding of fellowship. That was the purposed intention of man's very existence. We can see that in Scripture after Adam was created for a relational connection with God. That can be understood when He said that it wasn't good for man to be alone (Gen. 2:18). The bottom line reason for Eve to show up was in order for Adam to have someone to share life with. That in itself is a clear extension of what was already in place between Adam and his Creator. That progression is, as I see it, a continuation of the process of presence being enacted and sustained. God with Adam; Adam with Eve; and so on, and so on.

The purpose of that process is defined in Heb. 2:10, when

we're told that *"bringing many sons to glory"* was at the heart of why Christ came to earth. He came to make a way for relational fellowship to be restored after The Fall which broke the bond between God and humankind. The construction work on the bridge began just after the divide between the Creator and His creation took place. The completion of the entire bridge-work was finished on Golgotha at Calvary.

I believe that the content of Heb. 2:10 imparts a profound explanation of all of human history in regards to the restoration of relationship(s) between God and every person who has ever lived or will ever live on earth—at least potentially. When sin entered the world through man's disobedience to God's will, the relational distinctive between our Creator and us was broken (see Rom. 5:12-21). Thereafter God set in motion His plan for repairing the relational breach through sending Jesus *"in the fulness of the Godhead bodily"* (Col. 2:9). Each aspect of human history is therefore a component of that plan's fulfillment stated clearly and specifically in Heb. 2:10.

Processing "The Presence" contained and explained:

"It makes good sense that the God who got everything started and keeps everything going now completes the work by making the Salvation Pioneer perfect through suffering as he leads all these people to glory."

~Heb. 2:10-13 (MSG)

Yes and Amen.

A Pondering
TONGUE TROUBLES

"If you grow a healthy tree, you'll pick healthy fruit. If you grow a diseased tree, you'll pick worm-eaten fruit. The fruit tells you about the tree. You have minds like a snake pit! How do you suppose what you say is worth anything when you are so foul-minded? It's your heart, not the dictionary, that gives meaning to your words. A good person produces good deeds and words season after season. An evil person is a blight on the orchard. Let me tell you something: Every one of these careless words is going to come back to haunt you. There will be a time of reckoning. Words are powerful; take them seriously. Words can be your salvation. Words can also be your damnation."

~Mt. 12:33-37 (MSG)

Can you imagine how the followers of Christ (Christians, so called) could impact humanity if we understood the implications of the passage above? May God have mercy.

Paul says,

"You should not live like the unbelievers around you who walk in their empty delusions. Their corrupted logic has been clouded because their hearts are so far from God—their blinded understanding and deep-seated moral darkness keeps them from the true knowledge of God."
~Eph. 4:17–18 (TPT)

In Wayne-Speak: Spiritual ignorance comes from a hardness of heart regarding the ways of God and service in His kingdom. That in turn creates a darkened understanding of spiritual matters which leads to alienation from a godly life. Said simply, hardheartedness toward the will, way, and Word of God makes living a godly life virtually impossible. The end result is trash talk at its most damaging and perverse.

As followers of Christ, we are called to live and communicate from an entirely different perspective.

"So may the words of my mouth, my meditation-thoughts, and every movement of my heart be always pure and pleasing, acceptable before your eyes, my only Redeemer, my Protector-God."
~Ps. 19:14 (TPT)

There's a direct correlation between our words and our hearts in relationship to those passages. The KJV makes it very clear:

"O generation of vipers, how can ye, being evil, speak good things? for out of the abundance of the heart the mouth speaketh. A good man out of the good treasure of the heart bringeth forth good things: and an evil man out of the evil treasure bringeth forth evil things. But I say unto you, That

every idle word that men shall speak, they shall give account thereof in the day of judgment. For by thy words thou shalt be justified, and by thy words thou shalt be condemned."
~Mt. 12:34-37 (KJV)

Proverbs 18:21 (MSG) pushes the point even further stating,

"Words kill, words give life; they're either poison or fruit— you choose."

Those Scriptural directives each address the personal accountability that believers have to learn how to *"speak the truth in love"* (Eph. 4:15), *"bridle the tongue"* (Ja. 1:26–27), and to take this to heart:

"Whoever wants to embrace true life and find beauty in each day must stop speaking evil, hurtful words and never deceive in what they say. Always turn from what is wrong and cultivate what is good; eagerly pursue peace in every relationship, making it your prize. For the eyes of the Lord Yahweh rest upon the godly, and his heart responds to their prayers. But he turns his back on those who practice evil."
1 Pet. 3:10-12 (TPT)

A Biblical POV
HOPE
The Scriptural Antidote for Hopelessness

A lack of faith is caused by diminished hope.

"Faith is the substance of things hoped for…"
　　　　　　　　　　　　　　　　　　　　　～Heb. 11:1

Hope flows out of grace.

"Now may our Lord Jesus Christ Himself and God our Father, who has loved us and **given us** *eternal comfort and* **good hope by grace,** *comfort and strengthen your hearts in every good work and word."*
　　　　　　　　　　2 Thess.2:16 (emphasis mine)

Hopelessness is caused by an insufficient supply of grace. Grace is acquired from its source, which is located at the throne of grace.

"Therefore let us draw near with confidence to the throne of

grace, so that we may receive mercy and find grace to help in time of need."

~Heb. 4:12

To appropriate a fresh and increasing supply of grace, we should practice what Scripture says to do. That is the Biblical remedy for hopelessness and faithlessness which is becoming rampant throughout humanity. Simply stated, fresh grace renews hope, renewed hope manifests as faith, and faith introduces us to grace.

> *"Therefore, having been justified by faith, we have peace with God through our Lord Jesus Christ, through whom also we have obtained our* introduction by faith into this grace *in which we stand."*
>
> ~Rom. 5:1–2 (emphasis mine)

That process creates a Cycle of Hope. And free-flowing-ongoing-hope can then be appropriated as the antidote for overcoming hopelessness. A brief overview of how the Cycle works is this:

Faith is birthed by hope (Heb. 11:1); Hope flows out of grace (2 Thess. 2:16 and 1 Pet. 1:13); Grace is appropriated by going directly to the throne of grace in order to receive it (Heb. 4:16). A more detailed explanation of the Cycle of Hope is provided in the chapter "Channels Of Grace," found in my last book, *PONDERING(S) TOO*.

> *"Now may the Lord Jesus Christ and our Father God, who loved us and in his wonderful grace gave us eternal comfort and a beautiful hope that cannot fail, encourage your hearts*

and inspire you with strength to always do and speak what is good and beautiful in his eyes."
~2 Thess. 2:16–17 (TPT)

"Now our Lord Jesus Christ himself, and God, even our Father, which hath loved us, and hath given us everlasting consolation and good hope through grace, Comfort your hearts, and stablish you in every good word and work."
~2 Thess. 2:16–17 (KJV)

Notice that both translations say that grace and hope have been given to us by God. That is a past tense dynamic—done and done. That is to say that we, as followers of Christ, have already been given both things—grace and hope.

I believe that is speaking directly to the so-called first work of grace which is a gift given to every born again believer at the time of redemption.

"By grace are you saved, it is a gift of God."
~Eph. 2:5

The so-called second work of grace takes place on an ongoing basis if/when we choose to put Heb. 4:16 into action. The first work of grace is a gift freely given. The second work of grace is appropriated—meaning we have to request and then receive it.

One more thing: Notice the phrases above which say, *"always do and speak"* and *"every good work and word."* Both of those renderings speak of Paul's charge to all believers when he states,

"Whatever you do in word or deed, do all in the name of the

PARTICULAR PONDERING(S)

Lord Jesus, giving thanks through Him to God the Father."
~Col. 3:17

Selah…pause and consider.

A Biblical Perspective
PONDERING CIRCUMSTANCE

"Though the cherry trees don't blossom and the strawberries don't ripen, Though the apples are worm-eaten and the wheat fields stunted, Though the sheep pens are sheepless and the cattle barns empty, I'm singing joyful *praise to God. I'm turning cartwheels of joy to my Savior God. Counting on God's Rule to prevail, I take heart and gain strength. I run like a deer. I feel like I'm king of the mountain! (For congregational use, with a full orchestra.)"

~Hab. 3:17-19 (MSG)

*The word *praise* is "rejoice" (*alaz*) in the KJV. Based on the Hebrew definition it means to jump for joy.

Perhaps you don't have cherry trees in your back yard; strawberry plants in your garden; apple orchards, or wheat fields on your property; sheep pens for your sheep; barns for your cattle, horses, or produce. Your life circumstances may be more like this:

You didn't get the promotion or the bonus you were expecting at work. Or, the offer you made on the purchase of a new house was rejected. Or, the children you raised to live a certain way have turned out another way altogether. Or a relationship you said you couldn't live without fell apart. Or a healing or deliverance hasn't come when it was prayed for.

If any of those aspects of life, or any others that you felt were *sure things* haven't come to pass as you'd anticipated—Scripture challenges you to find fresh grace flowing from God's throne (Heb. 4:16), thereby acquiring new hope (1 Pet. 1:13). Then continue trying to walk out a life of faith (Heb. 11:1) in the name of and to the honor of the Lord, Christ Jesus (Col. 3:17), with praise indwelling you and manifesting out of you (1 Cor. 3:16), regardless of your present circumstances (Ja. 1:2-4).

Also see Ps. 84:5-7, Phil. 3:14 and 4:11.

A Testimony
DIVINE HAPPENSTANCE

September 15, 2017

Last Sunday, an amazing thing happened. Here's the short version:

Our new grandson (Benaiah Sibusiso Berry) attended his first worship service at just three weeks old. A family from Tampa was also in attendance. They were in our area having driven up from Florida to avoid the dangers of hurricane Irma. However, I think that the real reason they were there is that the Holy Ghost led them to our fellowship. During altar call, their family came forward directly toward me for prayer. When I finished praying for them, the father asked if he could meet my grandson.

I had given a brief testimony during the service regarding hearing from God through nature (Ps. 19:1-4 and Rom. 1:20). As I shared, I mentioned that Benaiah was "in the house" for the first time.

When we walked back to where our family was gathered, he asked if he could pray for the B-Boy. Of course we said yes. Then, this happened:

Before he prayed, he addressed us by explaining that he too, like Benaiah, was born of parents from two different nations. Then he laid hands on him and spoke a prophetic word that had to do with what he referred to as "dual nationality." Since our Sibusiso has an African mother and an American father, he said that his ability to move with a higher level of cultural discernment would take place in matters of interaction. Also, his ability to pray for others with a clearer focus regarding multi-racialism was in his future.

Personally, I believe that prayer has at its base two passages of Scripture that I've carried in my spirit for years. (See Ps. 2:8 and 2 Cor. 5:18-21)

May the Holy Ghost continue to open up the pathway into God's kingdom for this child, and for others through his witness and testimony as he grows into manhood.

A Pondering
WHY HUMANS?

"And God said, Let us make man in our image."
~Gen. 1:26 (KJV)

Ever ask yourself why? Well, I have. And this is what I came up with.

For relationship.

The very nature of the dynamic within and among the Trinity is that of relationship. The three persons of the Godhead are relational in their interaction with each other. So, the modeling of their companionship was worked out when the first human was fashioned—fashioned after their example as it were. We see that being further established in the provision of companionship that was given to Adam.

"God said, 'It's not good for the Man to be alone; I'll make him a helper, a companion.'"
~Gen. 2:18

Thereafter, the process of population continued, and does to this day. That's the basis for the *why* as I see it. Now consider the *how* with me.

Without going into an incredibly long, detailed, and extensive historical and theological discourse—which I am not qualified to do—I'll attempt a scaled down explanation of how the *why* has been worked out beginning at The Garden, when humankind first took up residence here on earth.

If the *why* was to establish the possibility of relationship with the Father, then how that was to be done had to take place. For that to transpire, a planned process was necessary. That plan began to manifest like this:

The Kingdom of God had to enter into earth's history and earth-time. For His Kingdom is *The Context* which into and out of flow all the contents of Christian spirituality. Since God's kingdom is eternal (without beginning, middle, or ending), the Creator of the universe established the concept of time on earth in order to interject (introduce) the very beginning of human history. That's what the very first line in the Bible tells us.

"In the beginning."

~Gen. 1:1

In the beginning of what? Of time.

That took place during the days of creation—morning and evening—day one—and so forth as presented in the Creation story (Gen. 1-3).

Thereafter, Adam and Eve became the first subjects (or citizens) of God's kingdom—here on earth as it is in heaven.

In order for a kingdom to function it requires four fundamental things:

1. A Ruler (God in Christ)
2. Subjects (those being ruled)
3. Rules (there was only one in The Garden. Others were to follow based on what took place after The Fall)
4. A place (domain) for the kingdom to manifest (on earth as it is in heaven)

All those components were in place prior to The Fall, as well as after it. That being the case, a major aspect of how relationships with the Father, Son, and Holy Ghost would then take place had to be set in motion. There had to be a way to restore the broken relationship between humans and God which would provide a way for relational restoration to happen. There was. It's called human history, and it arches across time, from The Fall in The Garden, all the way through to the return of Christ Jesus at The Second Coming. The entire history of humankind serves as a bridge positioned so that the goal of relationship with man, which the Trinity desired, could take place.

> *"What we actually see is Jesus, after being made temporarily inferior to the angels (and so subject to pain and death), in order that he should, in God's grace, taste death for every man, now crowned with glory and honor. It was right and proper that in bringing many sons to glory, God (from whom and by whom everything exists) should make the leader of their salvation a perfect leader through the fact that he suffered. For the one who makes men holy and the men who are made holy share a common humanity. So that he is not ashamed to call them his brothers, for he says: 'I will declare your name to my brethren; in the midst of the congregation I will sing praise to you.'"*
>
> ~Heb. 2:10-12 (Phillips)

I find that passage to be remarkable. What it conveys (in its scope and manifested outworking) is as profound as any other content found in Scripture. I find it odd that I've never heard it preached, or taught in a public presentation. Nor, as best as I can recall have I ever read any published material which addresses it. I find that baffling.

If I break it down, here's what it says to me:

Christ was brought to perfection (fullness, completeness) through the things He suffered. And the very reason that took place is clearly and profoundly stated in the text. The processing of His persecution and pain, crucifixion, death, burial, and resurrection took place in order for Him to be the Enabler, bringing many sons and daughters to glory! Christ Jesus became the bridge Himself whereby the reconciliation and restoration of the broken relationship between God and humankind could be renewed and re-established.

Jesus' life, offered in obedient service as a living sacrifice of worship (Rom. 12:1–2), was/is the Father's perfect plan for re-establishing connection between Himself (the Creator) and His creation from the moment of their personal redemption and then on into their eternal salvation and abiding relationship with the Trinity. *Amen*!

A Closing Caveat:

Grace is the unmerited favor of God's empowering presence, enabling me to be who He created me to be, so I can do what He calls me to do. (Wayne-Speak)

Note the use of grace in the passage below:

"But we see Jesus, who as a man, lived for a short time lower than the angels and has now been crowned with glorious honor because of what he suffered in his death. For it was

by God's grace that he experienced death's bitterness on behalf of everyone! *For now he towers above all creation, for all things exist through him and for him. And that God made him, pioneer of our salvation,* perfect (complete) through his sufferings…

…for this is how he brings many sons and daughters to share in his glory."

~Heb. 2:9–10 (TPT, emphasis mine)

"He's a bridge so let him take you over
He's a rock that's higher, higher than I
He's a way when there is no other
Jesus is, He's a bridge"

Fred Hammond

Ponderings and Postulations
FAITH

Scripture tells us what faith is: *"Faith is the substance of things hoped for, the evidence of things not seen."* (Heb. 11:1) That verse doesn't tell us what faith does. However, it does tell us what it is and where it comes from. Biblically speaking, it is the manifestation of hope in the lives of believers. It provides substantial evidence that it's available for use based on hope. In other words, the amount of faith we have to draw upon is directly linked to the amount of hope in us. Little hope, little faith—large hope, large faith. That being the case, for faith to be activate, hope must first be resident. Otherwise, it cannot be at work in the lives of those who are followers of Christ.

Five questions:

Where does hope come from? Hope flows from grace.

"Therefore, prepare your minds for action, keep sober in spirit, fix your hope completely on grace…"

~1 Pet. 1:13

Where does grace come from?

"God our Father, has given us eternal comfort and good hope by grace."
~2 Thess. 2:16

NOTE: That verse says that we've been given grace already (past tense). The grace being referred to there is what is commonly called "saving grace." Titus 2:11-13 says in part, *"For the grace of God has appeared (past tense), bringing salvation to all men…"* (emphasis added). Such "saving grace" comes at the point of conversion. It is a one-time gift so to speak. *"For by grace are we saved through faith…it is a gift from God"* (Eph. 2:8). Receiving God's initial grace gift in no way limits the potential for fresh, daily, ongoing grace to flow into our lives after redemption.

Is it possible to acquire grace on a regular and ongoing basis?

"Let us draw near with confidence to the throne of grace, so that we may receive mercy and find grace to help in time of need."
~Heb. 4:16

Can we also acquire grace on behalf of others? Heb. 4:16 tells us how we can receive grace for ourselves. It doesn't say that faith which is renewed (or increased) by coming before the throne of grace is for us alone. The way I read that verse, it appears to me that when we go boldly to request a grace-refill for ourselves, we can also request it for others who may be in need.

What is grace? Here's the working definition that I use: Grace is the unmerited favor of God's empowering presence, enabling me to be who He created me to be, so I can do what He calls me to do.

Selah…pause and consider.

A Pondering
LISTENING TO LANGUAGE

"The beauty of language set a hook in my soul."
~Bruce Cockburn

Mine too, Bruce.

"Starry-eyed and laughing as I recall when we were caught
Trapped by no track of hours for they hanged suspended
As we listened one last time and we watched with one last look
Spellbound and swallowed 'til the tolling ended
Tolling for the aching whose wounds cannot be nursed
For the countless confused, accused, misused, strung-out ones and worse
And for every hung-up person in the whole wide universe
And we gazed upon the chimes of freedom flashing"
(From: "Chimes Of Freedom Flashing" by Bob Dylan,
Audiam, Inc., used by permission)

A Pondering
BEING AND DOING

Acts 1:8 says in part that the disciples of Christ were/are to *be* witnesses. It does not say they are to *do* witnessing as such. Discipleship and evangelism (i.e. soul winning) are not the same thing. Evangelism helps lead/draw people to Christ. Discipleship teaches them how to grow into the character and nature of Christ—by being conformed into His image—*after* they're redeemed. (Rom. 8:29)

Witnesses offer their testimony through what they say and/or do. In order for a testimony to prove itself authentic, a witness has to have had an experience (or encounter) of which they can speak with veracity. Otherwise the witness himself/herself is considered as giving false testimony.

Selah…pause and consider.

A Biblical POV
KINGDOM CONSIDERATIONS

"Jesus didn't come to make a difference in the world, He came to make a different world."

~E. Stanley Jones

There's considerably more being stated in that sentence than you might notice at first reading. It appears to be a simple statement. But it isn't. At its essence, it explains why Jesus got so cross-ways with most of humanity when He began His ministry here on earth.

The "different world" which Jones mentions is referring to an entirely other way of life being lived. That otherness has a name—it's the kingdom of God.

> "Jesus looked at Pilate and said, 'The royal power of my kingdom realm doesn't come from this world. If it did, then my followers would be fighting to the end to defend me from the Jewish leaders. My kingdom realm authority is not from this realm.'"
>
> ~Jn. 18:36 (TPT)

When Jesus began to clarify why He was here and what

His intentions were, He upset every man-made system that was currently in operation. Governments, religions, cultural customs, social dynamics, and such were all being confounded with the prospects of an entirely different way of functioning. He was ushering in a wholly/holy other way of living. The result of such potential lifestyle adjustments throughout all of humankind as to how things were being done was confusion, chaos, frustration, hostility, and anger. The fallout from such profoundly bold utterances of the Lord is still as challenging today, personally and corporately, as it was when Christ made His first declaration(s) regarding the new world order He was sent to usher in.

Quoting again from the book, *The Unshakable Kingdom And The Unchangeable Person* by E. Stanley Jones:

"The two most important things Jesus ever spoke, the Lord's Prayer and the Beatitudes, both began with the kingdom of God. And the most important thing He said in the Sermon on the Mount was" 'Seek first ye the kingdom of God…and all things shall be added unto you.' So first and last and between times the emphasis is upon the kingdom of God. And not a marginal emphasis, but the organizing emphasis upon which everything revolved and from which everything gets its meaning."

Jesus said of Himself and His ministry,

"I must tell the good news of the kingdom of God to other towns as well—that is my mission."
~Luke 4:43 (Phillips)

The very coming of Christ, His embodiment on earth, was intended and purposed to turn the world as it was upside down and inside out. His life's objective was to manifest, model, and implement the way the Father's kingdom was designed to operate. In fact, He gave His life to accomplish that. That's what "*It is finished*" means.

> *"After this, Jesus realizing that everything was now completed said (fulfilling the saying of scripture), 'I am thirsty.' There was a bowl of sour wine standing there. So they soaked a sponge in the wine, put it on a spear, and pushed it up towards his mouth. When Jesus had taken it, he cried, 'It is finished!' His head fell forward, and he died."*
> ~Jn. 19:28-30 (Phillips)

Humanity at large, and the body of Christ in general is still trying to sort out the *whys, hows,* and *whens* of all that. As I survey the current conditions of life here on the planet, it appears to me that the implementation of God's kingdom isn't going very well. My personal perspective is now (and for the rest of my life) based on what Jesus said was to be the first and foremost priority for those who are following after Him.

> *"Seek first the kingdom of God and His righteousness…"*
> ~Mt. 6:33

Based on my understanding of Scripture, I don't believe that charge has ever been lifted or countermanded. It is still what Christians are called to do—represent God's kingdom, today, tomorrow, and all the way over Jordan.

Heaven on Earth
THY KINGDOM COME

What follows is a brief discussion between a mother and her 4 year old son regarding the recent death of his grandmother:

Son: *I miss grandmother.*
Mom: *So do I son.*
Son: *I know she's in heaven.*
Mom: *That's right.*
Son: *I wish heaven could be on earth.*
Mom: *Me too. Wouldn't that be wonderful.*
Son: *Yeah. If heaven were on earth it would swallow up everything else.*

I believe the son's closing comment is one of the most profound theological statements regarding the Kingdom of God that I've ever heard. Did I mention that he's only four years old?

> *"From the mouths of children and infants You have ordained praise on account of Your adversaries, to silence the enemy and avenger."*
>
> ~Ps. 8:2 (Berean Study Bible)

PARTICULAR PONDERING(S)

"For the earth will be filled with the knowledge of the glory of the Lord, as the waters cover the sea."
~Hab. 2:14 (NASB)

"Now, I tell you this, my brothers and sisters, flesh and blood are not able to inherit God's kingdom realm, and neither will that which is decaying be able to inherit what is incorruptible. Listen, and I will tell you a divine mystery: not all of us will die, but we will all be transformed. It will happen in an instant—in the twinkling of his eye. For when the last trumpet is sounded, the dead will come back to life. We will be indestructible and we will be transformed. For we will discard our mortal 'clothes' and slip into a body that is imperishable. What is mortal now will be exchanged for immortality. And when that which is mortal puts on immortality, and what now decays is exchanged for what will never decay, then the Scripture will be fulfilled that says:

Death is swallowed up by a triumphant victory. So death, tell me, where is your victory? Tell me death, where is your sting?
~1 Cor. 15:50-57 (TPT)

I encourage you to experience the song: "Heaven On Earth" by David and Nicole Binion. You can watch it online on YouTube and similar platforms.

Pondering Grace
RECEIVING AND GIVING

The Holy Ghost has given me a new prayer to offer up for others. It's this: May God grace you with hope. Follow please…

"Let us therefore come boldly unto the throne of grace, that we may obtain mercy, and find grace to help in time of need."
~Heb. 4:16 (KJV)

That text clearly states that followers of Christ can/should come "boldly before the throne of grace" in order to receive help for themselves in time of need. However, it does not restrict/limit those who come—on their own behalf—from requesting extra portion(s) of grace to extend to others in their time(s) of need. So, over the last several months I've been praying that way—grace for myself and for others as well.

I'll insert my *working definition of grace here for the sake of clarity:

Grace is the unmerited favor of God's empowering presence, enabling me to be who He created me to be, so I can do what He calls me to do.

*A working definition is what I use when I'm referring to (teaching) a specific topic.

This process of requesting grace, for myself and others, has in turn birthed the prayer I mentioned at the beginning of this post: May God grace you with hope. I encourage you to try it yourself.

Lastly, consider these two verses in light of what I've just stated:

> "May the Lord Jesus Christ and God our Father (who has loved us and given us unending encouragement and unfailing hope by his grace) inspire you with courage and confidence in every good thing you say or do."
> ~2 Thess. 2:16-17 (Phillips)

Note the phrase, "hope by his grace."

> "Therefore, preparing your minds for action, and being sober-minded, set your hope fully on the grace that will be brought to you at the revelation of Jesus Christ."
> ~1 Pet. 1:13 (ESV)

Note the phrase "set your hope fully on the grace."

Selah…pause and consider.

For consideration, here's another passage which offers an example of how something we appropriate for ourselves can then in turn be passed along to others.

"Thank God, the Father of our Lord Jesus Christ, that he is

our Father and the source of all mercy and comfort. For he gives us comfort in our trials so that we in turn may be able to give the same sort of strong sympathy to others in theirs. Indeed, experience shows that the more we share Christ's suffering the more we are able to give of his encouragement. This means that if we experience trouble we can pass on to you comfort and spiritual help; for if we ourselves have been comforted we know how to encourage you to endure patiently the same sort of troubles that we have ourselves endured. We are quite confident that if you have to suffer troubles as we have done, then, like us, you will find the comfort and encouragement of God."

~2 Cor. 1:3–4 (Phillips)

The process of passing along comfort is (I believe) exactly the same as passing along grace (Heb. 4:16). It is, after all, better to give than to receive (Acts 20:35).

AAA
APPROXIMATED ANECDOTAL AXIOM

There's grace, beauty, and inherent joy in the extravagant. But far too often the ordinary doesn't discern, appreciate, or appropriate it. As a result, humankind tends to defer to the ordinary as its collective-default-setting. Our common loss is fulfillment of the potential of promise.

"I'm pressing on to the mark of the higher calling of my Lord."
~Phil. 3:14

Selah...pause and consider.

An Analogy
COMPUTING THE KINGDOM

Think of yourself (body, soul, mind, and spirit) as a computer. The Kingdom of God (KOG) is the operating system you were made to properly function with. Although it is possible to use an alternate operating system, it will malfunction over and over again. As a result of running on the wrong system, it will crash repeatedly, until reaching a point where rebooting is no longer an option. Your entire system will be—fried.

The Bible is intended to be your manual of operation. It contains any and all information necessary for keeping your computer properly maintained. It is loaded up with all the resources (principles, precepts, commandments, status, testimonies, ordinances, rules, laws, and words) required to do all the system was designed to do—by the Manufacturer (see Ps. 119). Each one of those components is a type of software program intended to inter-face with the KOG to accomplish everything it was designed (created) to do. (See Ps. 139:14 and 2 Pet. 1:2–11.)

Once you've unpacked all the equipment, the first step thereafter is to plug it into its power source in order for it to work.

The source is *grace. That's where the power comes from for starting it up and for ongoing performance. (See Heb. 4:16.)

*Grace is the unmerited favor of God's empowering presence, enabling us to be who He created us to be, so that we can do what He calls us to do.

"Seek first the kingdom of God..."

~Mt. 6:33

Selah...pause and consider.

A Pondering
THE PROCESS OF PROCESSING

In May of '17, I entered the retirement phase of my life. Having a personal dislike for the negative charge that the word *retirement* carries, I quickly replaced it with the word *rebootment*. A term with a little more contemporary energy.

Then In March of '18, the Holy Ghost gave me an entirely different perspective to begin working through. It has to do with setting (or re-setting) my personal spiritual priorities related directly to Mt. 6:33 which states in part, *"Seek first the Kingdom of God and His righteous…"* So, since then I've been on the sojourning along the pathway of recalibration. Here's one thing I've learned so far:

It's pretty amazing what can happen in terms of hearing the voice of the Lord when you take, make, or have the time to listen with more intentionality. It's not that His voice changed. Rather, my ability to listen has. Two verses which have been life-giving to me for years have now grown in significance over these last months of recalibration.

"I know now how to live when things are difficult and I know how to live when things are prosperous. In general and in

particular I have learned the secret of facing either poverty or plenty. I am ready for anything through the strength of the one who lives within me."

~Phil. 4:11-13 (Phillips)

"Let every activity of your lives and every word that comes from your lips be drenched with the beauty of our Lord Jesus, the Anointed One. And bring your constant praise to God the Father because of what Christ has done for you!"

~Col. 3:17 (TPT)

That's it for now.

A Pondering
PERFORMANCE vs. PERFORMANCE

Soren Kierkegaard, a Danish philosopher in the 19th century, once clarified the most common misconception about worship using the analogy of a drama.

"When we come to worship God, we generally feel as though the preacher and other ministers are the performers and God is the subject of the performance and we as the congregation are merely the audience—but this is a terrible misunderstanding of worship."

Kierkegaard is describing a consumer-oriented approach, focused more on what we receive than what we give. He goes on to say, "Authentic Christian worship is just the opposite. We, the congregation, are the performers. The preachers and other ministers are the directors of the performance and God is the audience."

Oct. 29, 20011 / rightfromtheheart.org

We are performers *in* the house, not *for* the house.

"Since Eden mankind has been striving to "become something" beyond an earthling. We want to "make a name for ourselves" like the people building the Tower of Babel. We want to be noticed and appreciated by others. We are in competition with one another for prestige. We see others as superior (because we think we are lacking in some way) and we want to be like them, nay, even better than them. We reject others (like Cain did Abel) so we can thrive. Jesus refused to play our game; he gave himself to Father's will in Gethsemane."

~Fount Shults

AN AUDIENCE OF ONE

A room within a room am I, a world within the world outside
Hidden from the eyes of men, I'm your secret
Most of life is lived inside, in visions of the soul and mind
Don't want to waste this sacred space, when You're in it

Chorus

I am Your cathedral, in the midst of the people
In the congregation, life is lived
Before the audience of One
Everything I say and do, every little part of me
You see the silent conversations in my head
You see me when I rise, I fall
My God, my God, you see it all
Every dream I dream while on my bed

A room within a room am I, a world within the world outside
You fill me with Your glory, then you break out
A tabernacle filled with You, a riverbed that flows into

PERFORMANCE vs. PERFORMANCE

The desert of this broken world, God break out
Break out, break out, break out

Repeat Chorus

Misty Edwards and Paul Moak
Forerunner Worship/Misty Edwards Music, used by permission

Anywhere, Any Time
THE SECURITY OF SANCTUARY DISCOVERY
(Jonah's Story)

I know you likely know the story of Jonah pretty well. But perhaps not quite as well as you think you do. So here's an overview that may detail the events of the narrative with a little more depth than you've ever considered.

Right here at the top I'll state that my intention is to show you how Omnipresence works and how understanding it can impact any life, anywhere at any time.

I'm not going to unpack the entire story. Rather, I'll just establish a limited context in order to focus in on one particular portion of the events presented to us scripturally.

To begin: Jehovah places a charge before Jonah that He wants taken care of. Jonah objects to the job assignment and decides to run away from God's presence. That right there is the first theological issue in the narrative. How's that? Because it's impossible to run away (remove) yourself from Omnipresence. To be Omnipresent is to be everywhere all the time. Jonah doesn't know or understand that to be the case—at least not yet. So he continues with his ill-considered escape plan. To continue…

He books passage on a boat that's headed for parts unknown, as the story unfolds:

Jonah goes below deck and proceeds to fall asleep. Then a huge storm blows in, seemingly from out of nowhere. Some see that as Divine wrath or judgement toward Jonah for his disobedience. I see it as a Divine wake up call. Remember Jonah is asleep in the lower deck and God needs him top side in order for the story to progress toward its climax. Hence, the storm is there to shake and stir him awake—along with everyone else on board.

I'll insert a reminder here of what Jehovah's original charge was to Jonah. He was to travel to Nineveh and evangelize the entire city. He was to walk through the city as a living witness and give testimony through evangelism to the citizens living there. Now, back to the boat, the storm, and the all-hands-on-deck scene which is beginning to unfold.

The crew is in a panic! Even though they are all seasoned sailors, they are frightened by a storm unlike any they have ever had the misfortune of trying to navigate through. Every time they try to distance themselves from its fury, it seems to increase in intensity, as if it were being controlled by some unseen (or unknown) force, which it is.

Although they are not God-fearing men, they are nonetheless aware of the gods, believing that they have the ability to affect and influence circumstances on earth. Note please there is a distinct difference between *God* with a capital *G*, and *gods* with a lowercase *g* and an *s*, designating a plural tense. (See Deut. 5:7). The big G *God* is the only "One True God." The little g *god(s)* are not Him. That's a very important Biblical fact to take to heart. It was true then, and it is still true today.

After a time of extended struggle to escape the storm, the

consensus is that every man on board should call upon his own god for mercy and deliverance. They see that as their only hope for survival. The dynamic in this scene changes radically when Jonah makes the following declaration:

> *"I am a Hebrew, and I fear the Lord God of heaven who made the sea and the dry land."*
>
> ~Jonah 1: 9

The crew's fear and apprehension is now maximized having been informed that the God of creation is the One who Jonah is trying to run away from. What follows next appears to be an impassioned climax. However it is really just an increase in tension meant to set up what's about to take place next—which is where I'm headed with these observations.

Jonah tells the crewmen that they should throw him overboard, which in turn will likely bring the storm to an abrupt end, thereby saving their lives. If you've never noticed what's taking place here, please consider these two points specifically:

Jonah's explanation regarding his God, who He was, and what He's capable of is a testimony, and is in fact an act of evangelism—which was directly related to Jehovah's charge to Jonah to begin with.

Jonah is asking the crewmembers to commit an act of murder!

Here's an amazing by-product of what's taken place so far in this narrative.

Their response to Jonah's request is clearly stated as follows:

> *"However, the men rowed desperately to return to land but they could not, for the sea was becoming even stormier against them. Then they called on the Lord and said, 'We earnestly*

pray, O Lord, do not let us perish on account this man's life and do not put innocent blood on us; for You, O Lord, have done as You have pleased.'"

~Jonah 1:13–14 (KJV)

Jonah's solution for resolving their quandary prompted a boat filled with unbelievers to call upon a God they had no personal understanding of by turning/calling on Him for their rescue and deliverance. I see that as a form of repentance, which in turn may have led them to conversion and redemption. That's an amazing encounter to comprehend, prompted by a request from a man fleeing from his God and requesting that people he barely even knew become murderers in order to save their own lives. To me, that's overwhelming to ponder. But all that is merely a set up for what's about to happen.

I'll provide the script for what happens next directly from the KJV. It is, to me, one of the most poetically descriptive passages in Scripture:

"Then Jonah prayed unto the Lord his God out of the fish's belly, and said, 'I cried by reason of mine affliction unto the Lord, and he heard me; out of the belly of hell cried I, and thou heardest my voice. For thou hadst cast me into the deep, in the midst of the seas; and the floods compassed me about: all thy billows and thy waves passed over me. Then I said, I am cast out of thy sight; yet I will look again toward thy holy temple.

The waters compassed me about, even to the soul: the depth closed me round about, the weeds were wrapped about my head. I went down to the bottoms of the mountains; the earth with her bars was about me forever: yet hast thou brought up my life from corruption, O Lord my God. When my soul fainted within me I remembered the Lord: and my prayer came in unto thee, into thine holy temple.

They that observe lying vanities forsake their own mercy. But I will sacrifice unto thee with the voice of thanksgiving; I will pay that that I have vowed. Salvation is of the Lord. And the Lord spake unto the fish, and it vomited out Jonah upon the dry land."

~Jonah 2, emphasis mine

Chapter 2 contains data that most people who read it rarely (if ever) grasp in terms of context and importance. Here's why: All of chapter 2 is a remembrance by Jonah focused on what took place *after* he was thrown overboard. Consider this:

The "fish" was not his punishment for disobedience. It was his deliverance from drowning. God's mercy made provision for His wayward child which resulted in the narrative that Jonah shares of his personal and potential death. Here's how his recollections are explained from his personal experience:

First of all I'll deal with the issue of water. In specific, the sea which Jonah has been thrown into. Any body of water (streams, rivers, ponds, lakes, oceans) are all contained (or located) on earth. That is to say earth is the foundation which holds various bodies of water in place. Said another way, earth is the container in/on which water is held. That's important to keep in mind as Jonah begins to explain his perspective on what he'd been through.

He says that the waters covered him, and that their depths surrounded him. He was engulfed. Then he says that seaweed was wrapped around his neck, making his eminent death even

THE SECURITY OF SANCTUARY DISCOVERY

more extreme as he struggled to free himself. He continues by stating that he went down to the bottom of the mountains. That's why I've mentioned that water has at its base the earth which it covers. Jonah is saying that he went down to the bottom of the water where the mountains have their roots (or their foundational base).

Note that his recollection of drowning which he is sharing is based on what he recalls was taking place—in real time—as he was sinking down in the depths. That is to say he knew what was happening and had no way of escaping what clearly appeared to be his demise. The next thing he says is a major moment in the story. He declares, *"yet hast thou brought up my life from corruption, O Lord my God. When my soul fainted within me I remembered the Lord: and my prayer came in unto thee, into thine holy temple."*

See that statement as taking place at the precise moment he was about to die. God's hand of deliverance was there just in the nick of time so to speak. At death's watery door, he's moved from death by drowning directly into survival in the belly of a fish. Now we've arrived at the main point of my presentation.

Look again at the opening verses of Jonah's recollections. He tells us that his prayer took place while he was in the belly of the fish. In that context, consider this:

He was taken out of certain death by drowning and transported directly into an environment he had no way of comprehending. Here's what that environment would have been like:

- Total darkness
- A stench too strong to imagine
- Anywhere he touched would have been covered with slime

He had no way to secure or steady himself if the place/thing containing him were to move—which it most certainly would have—fish swim.

He would have had no way to determine where he was or how he got there.

He had absolutely no way of knowing if he would survive in the state he was in. He was saved from drowning only to become fish food.

Nonetheless, in that unimaginable place, Jonah prayed a prayer of thanksgiving. In doing so, he converted his current condition and circumstance into a living sanctuary—a high and holy temple—in the very Presence of God! (Read chapter 2 again for context and clarity.)

As I said at the beginning of my narrative, there is no place that an Omnipresent God isn't. As His people, we should all try much harder to remember that anywhere we are, and at any time we are there—so is He.

A Pondering
NEVER LOSE YOUR SONG

"Along the banks of Babylon's rivers we sat as exiles, mourning our captivity, and wept with great love for Zion. Our music and mirth were no longer heard, only sadness. We hung up our harps on the willow trees.

Our captors tormented us, saying, 'Make music for us and sing one of your happy Zion-songs!' But how could we sing the song of the Lord in this foreign wilderness?"

~Ps. 137:1-4 (TPT)

To share my thoughts on the passage above, I'll turn it around in order to consider it from a different perspective. First I want to offer a disclaimer: I mean no disrespect to the saints mentioned in it. I cannot state for certain how I would have reacted had I been in the situation they found themselves in. Really, I don't know if anyone can say for certain what they'd do if they were led into captivity by their enemies. Circumstances such as that can shake a person's commitment and personal resolve in matters of faith down to the core. Such was clearly the nature of those described in the scene presented

PARTICULAR PONDERING(S)

in the text. In the state they were in, they did ask a question that needs answering. That's what I'm responding to.

Their question was, *"...how shall we sing the Lord's song in a strange land?"*

Before I provide an answer to that, I'll examine the particulars which prompted the question to begin with.

The context for the narrative is as follows: *"By the rivers of Babylon, there we sat down, yes, we wept, when we remembered Zion."* (KJV)

Having been taken captive, and carried from their homeland to a foreign wilderness, they found themselves prisoners—brokenhearted and in despair for how things once were. Longing for home.

Due to the dark and desperate conditions they were in they were not able to process their circumstances in the moment—in real time. Rather, they were caught up in their memories of what had been, rendering them incapable of addressing their current reality from a position of strong faith. Their loss had been too great. As a result they found themselves hopeless. Once hopelessness sets in, it is virtually impossible to muster up any faith at all. Why? Because faith itself flows directly from hope.

"Faith is the substance of things hoped for, the evidence of things not seen."

~Heb. 11:1

Little hope, little faith. Their dire and dismal environment had drained all their hope out until none was left for faith to manifest from. That is to say, what they saw, what they were experiencing, was overriding their ability to respond through faith. To clarify: Faith could not—does not—manifest where there is a lack of hope. It cannot. In order for the substance of faith to in fact become evident, it must have a source. And, according to Heb. 11:1, the source of faith is one thing, and one thing only—Hope.

Their joy and gladness, their praise and proclamation (testimony) had been stolen away by their captors and the condition in which they were placed. The initial result was that their song(s) had also been stolen along with their freedom. So, the instruments of worship and praise which they had been allowed to bring with them were no longer of any use. (See 2 Chron. 29:26–27.) They just surrendered them as well by hanging them up on the willow trees.

Based on how the scene unfolds, it's clear that their captors took advantage of their lost ability to offer up praise when they said sarcastically, *"Sing for us one of the songs of Zion."* (v.3c)

Watch this: The testimony of God's people through the singing of their songs had resounded throughout the region *prior* to them even being brought there. How else would their enemies have known to taunt them by requesting that they sing a song of Zion if they hadn't already been aware that such songs (and singers, and musicians) existed? The power of proclaimed praise reaches much further than the place they are offered up from. They have a spiritual energy embedded in them which can impact untold locations and those who occupy them. (See also 1 Thess. 1:1-8.)

NOTE: See the blog entries entitled "Worship On The Wind" (Parts 1 and 2 in section one of this book.)

All I've shared here brings us to the question which had been posed regarding the inability to sing when freedom is seemingly no longer available. In order to provide an answer to that question, please ponder the following two examples from both the Old and New Testament. I believe they provide Scripturally-Biblical responses.

I'm including the entire story because it's such a fantastic read. Apply as needed.

> *"Sometime later the Moabites and Ammonites, accompanied by Meunites, joined forces to make war on Jehoshaphat. Jehoshaphat received this intelligence report: "A huge force is on its way from beyond the Dead Sea to fight you. There's no time to waste—they're already at Hazazon Tamar, the oasis of En Gedi." Shaken, Jehoshaphat prayed. He went to God for help and ordered a nationwide fast. The country of Judah united in seeking God's help—they came from all the cities of Judah to pray to God.*
>
> *"Then Jehoshaphat took a position before the assembled people of Judah and Jerusalem at The Temple of God in front of the new courtyard and said, "O God, God of our ancestors, are you not God in heaven above and ruler of all kingdoms below? You hold all power and might in your fist—no one stands a chance against you! And didn't you make the natives of this land leave as you brought your people Israel in, turning it over permanently to your people Israel, the descendants of Abraham your friend? They have lived here and built a holy house of worship to honor you, saying, 'When the worst happens—whether war or flood or disease or famine—and we take our place before this Temple (we know you are personally present in this place!) and pray out our pain and trouble, we know that you will listen and give victory.' "And now it's happened: men from Ammon, Moab, and Mount Seir have shown up. You didn't let Israel touch them when we got here at first—we detoured around them*

and didn't lay a hand on them. And now they've come to kick us out of the country you gave us. O dear God, won't you take care of them? We're helpless before this vandal horde ready to attack us. We don't know what to do; we're looking to you."

"Everyone in Judah was there—little children, wives, sons—all present and attentive to God. Then Jahaziel was moved by the Spirit of God to speak from the midst of the congregation. (Jahaziel was the son of Zechariah, the son of Benaiah, the son of Jeiel, the son of Mattaniah the Levite of the Asaph clan.) He said, "Attention everyone—all of you from out of town, all you from Jerusalem, and you King Jehoshaphat—God's word: Don't be afraid; don't pay any mind to this vandal horde. This is God's war, not yours. Tomorrow you'll go after them; see, they're already on their way up the slopes of Ziz; you'll meet them at the end of the ravine near the wilderness of Jeruel. You won't have to lift a hand in this battle; just stand firm, Judah and Jerusalem, and watch God's saving work for you take shape. Don't be afraid, don't waver. March out boldly tomorrow—God is with you."

"Then Jehoshaphat knelt down, bowing with his face to the ground. All Judah and Jerusalem did the same, worshiping God. The Levites (both Kohathites and Korahites) stood to their feet to praise God, the God of Israel; they praised at the top of their lungs! They were up early in the morning, ready to march into the wilderness of Tekoa. As they were leaving, Jehoshaphat stood up and said, "Listen Judah and Jerusalem! Listen to what I have to say! Believe firmly in God, your God, and your lives will be firm! Believe in your prophets and you'll come out on top!"

"After talking it over with the people, Jehoshaphat appointed a choir for God; dressed in holy robes, they were to march

PARTICULAR PONDERING(S)

ahead of the troops, singing, "Give thanks to God, His love never quits."

"As soon as they started shouting and praising, God set ambushes against the men of Ammon, Moab, and Mount Seir as they were attacking Judah, and they all ended up dead. The Ammonites and Moabites mistakenly attacked those from Mount Seir and massacred them. Then, further confused, they went at each other, and all ended up killed. As Judah came up over the rise, looking into the wilderness for the horde of barbarians, they looked on a killing field of dead bodies—not a living soul among them.

"When Jehoshaphat and his people came to carry off the plunder they found more loot than they could carry off— equipment, clothing, valuables. It took three days to cart it away! On the fourth day they came together at the Valley of Blessing (Beracah) and blessed God (that's how it got the name, Valley of Blessing). Jehoshaphat then led all the men of Judah and Jerusalem back to Jerusalem—an exuberant parade. God had given them joyful relief from their enemies! They entered Jerusalem and came to The Temple of God with all the instruments of the band playing. When the surrounding kingdoms got word that God had fought Israel's enemies, the fear of God descended on them. Jehoshaphat heard no more from them; as long as Jehoshaphat reigned, peace reigned."

~2 Chron. 20 (MSG)

The story speaks for itself. It stands as a perfect example of how praise can be offered up in any set of circumstances.

Praise is always in order! Can I get an amen?

"A great crowd gathered, and all the people joined in to come

against them. The Roman officials ordered that Paul and Silas be stripped of their garments and beaten with rods on their bare backs. After they were severely beaten, they were thrown into prison and the jailer was commanded to guard them securely. So the jailer placed them in the innermost cell of the prison and had their feet bound and chained. Paul and Silas, undaunted, prayed in the middle of the night and sang songs of praise to God, while all the other prisoners listened to their worship. Suddenly, a great earthquake shook the foundations of the prison. All at once every prison door flung open and the chains of all the prisoners came loose."
~Acts 16:22-26 (TPT)

There you have two testimonies which clearly model examples of how the proclamations of praise can be offered up when there is no reasonable justification for a sacrifice of worship to be brought forth. Well, there is one reason:

"I will bless the Lord at all times: his praise shall continually be in my mouth."
~Ps. 34:1 (KJV)

A Pondering
THE SHAPE OF DESTINY

Webster's DictionaryDefinition of *destiny*:
1. something to which a person or thing is destined : fortune wants to control his own *destiny*
2. a predetermined course of events often held to be an irresistible power or agency felt that *destiny* would determine their future

Christian Definition of Destiny: A strong belief in a supernatural power or powers that control human destiny. An institution to express belief in a divine power. A belief concerning the supernatural, sacred, or divine, and the practices and institutions associated with such belief. The sum total of answers given to explain humankind's relationship with the universe.

What I'm about to share here is intended for those who are followers of Christ. Individuals who are born again, saved, the redeemed of the Lord. For the sake of this article, I am not addressing—or concerned with—those who do not consider themselves to be part of the body of Christ, or the church-at-large.

Within the fellowship of believers over the last 25 years or so, I've noticed what I consider to be a misappropriation of what destiny is and what it means. During that general span of time, it appears to have become a term which is now biased toward the positive. By that I mean that many so called believers seem to understand destiny as being something which can only be considered as singularly beneficial for those who are "in Christ." A sort of entitlement program that comes as a guarantee with salvation.

Let me be as clear as possible: There *is* an eternally destined guarantee for those who are in and of the faith. However, eternal promises do not necessarily manifest while living temporally here on earth. Our lives are as a shadow which passes away (Ps. 144:4). Whereas the eternal destiny of the believer is, well, eternal.

Such a predisposition toward a positive destiny for Christians means that their future on a temporal level is based on personal entitlement through their relational union with Christ. In other words, as long as life here on earth is working well, then destiny is being biblically fulfilled. If however, the hopes, plans, dreams, and aspirations aren't coming to pass, the enemy has somehow stolen away the Divine plan for their lives. Such a perspective theologically can create all sorts of problems for those who see their future as only positive—by God's grand design for their lives.

Viewed from the sole perspective of positivity, life becomes a black and white process. If things are going good, then God's plan of Divine destiny is working unhindered. If however, things aren't working out as *we* planned they would, then Satan has one way or another derailed the future. When that happens, you can find yourself operating with a misconception like this:

"And we know that God causes all *good* things to work for good for those who love God, to those who are called according to His purpose." (Rom. 8:28)

FYI: The word *good* inserted prior to the word *things* isn't in that verse folks.

"We were created to participate with God in bringing creation forward to its intended destiny. "Subdue the earth" means bring it under the rule of the God of love. Jurgen Moltmann suggested that we were given authority as the "justice of the peace" over God's creation. That's why Jesus called the peacemakers blessed, "for they shall be called sons of God" (Mt. 5:9). Sons and daughters who do what they see Father doing participate with him in bringing his kingdom to earth."

~Fount Shults

I could attempt to provide a considerable amount of detail in regards to what I am trying to get at, but I'll just cite three brief examples from Scripture and leave it at that.

#1: In the matter of Sovereignty, *"…we are the clay and You are the potter; and all of us are the work of Your hands."* (Is. 64:8) See also Romans 9:21 which says, *"Or does not the potter have a right over the clay…"*

#2: Paul states, *"…I count all things to be loss in view of the surpassing value of knowing Christ Jesus my Lord, for whom I have suffered the loss of all things, and count them but rubbish so that I may gain Christ…"* (Phil. 3:8).

When Paul says he counts *"all things as loss"* he's combining things good as well as bad. In other words, the dynamics of a positive or negative impact of what's happened to him as he lived out his life was considered as nothing when compared to the worth of his eternal destiny with God in Christ. That is to say, his heavenly rewards were of greater value to him than *anything* here on earth. His destiny was based on his hope in Christ.

"If the only benefit of our hope in Christ is limited to this life on earth, we deserve to be pitied more than all others! (1 Cor. 15:19, TPT)

#3: *"Women received back their dead by resurrection; and others were tortured, not accepting their release, so that they might obtain a better resurrection; and others experienced mockings and scourgings, yes, also chains and imprisonment. They were stoned, they were sawn in two, they were tempted, they were put to death with the sword; they went about in sheepskins, in goatskins, being destitute, afflicted, ill-treated (men of whom the world was not worthy), wandering in deserts and mountains and caves and holes in the ground. And all these, having gained approval through their faith, did not receive what was promised, because God had provided something better for us, so that apart from us they would not be made perfect."* (Heb. 11:35-40, NASB)

As I read that passage I notice the following:

The saints mentioned are nameless. They are of "no reputation" (Phil. 2:5-11). The writer of Hebrews says that of them *"the world was not worthy."* That's an astounding thing to say regarding a people who aren't even named personally for their lives offered up to their God. They all died having not received what was promised to them. At least not here on earth.

If those three passages don't serve to help you gain a clear biblical basis for how you see your destiny—I doubt that anything else I might say would be of any more help.

There is this as well: *"Though he slay me, I will hope in him…"* (Job 13:15a, ESV). I recommend "Though You Slay Me" by Shane & Shane—The story behind the song at:

https://www.youtube.com/watch?v=bETuP57T_90

A Pondering
SEED SOWING

> *"Those who sow in tears shall reap with shouts of joy! He who goes out weeping, bearing the seed for sowing, shall come home with shouts of joy, bringing his sheaves with him."*
> ~Ps. 126:5–6 (ESV)

That passage is fundamentally about ministry—evangelism really. There are several aspects to it which are implied by the language more than they are stated. This is my take on that.

Firstly, there are two ways to understand the opening line regarding sowing in tears.

It could be saying that whatever type of seed is being sown, it could be that tears may be necessary as the sowing is taking place.

It could also be saying that the seed itself consists of tears. More poetic, but certainly possible.

Either way works for me.

In the parable of the sower (Mt. 13), we're told that the seed is the Word of God. So from a Biblical standpoint that's an appropriate way to understand the phrase regarding the sowing of seed itself. That being the case, for someone to be able to sow the Word, they would have to have seed available. I'd call that being "Word-friendly." That is to say, carrying the Word-seed with you to plant would require you to have it with you—or perhaps in you as the case may be. You cannot sow seed which you do not possess, or steward. So in order to fulfill the narrative of the text in regards to sowing seed, one must have at the very least some seed to sow. No seed, no sowing. Little seed, little sowing. Lots of seed, lots of sowing. I see that as an important principle for consideration.

The second point, on the other hand, comes from a place which is rarely a topic of discourse in the so-called contemporary church anymore. It has to do with the practice of lamenting—or if you will, lamentation. I'll provide some definitions to help clarify what I have to say.

Lament (Webster's Dictionary): A crying out in grief; wailing; a dirge.

Lamentation (Webster's): An act or instance of lamenting.

Lament (From the Hebrew / Strong's Concordance): To tear the hair and beat the breast. To mourn. (From the Greek): To bewail. From a word meaning to wail. From a word meaning to clamor.

Lamentation (From the Greek): A dirge. From a word meaning to strike a musical note (i.e. to chant or wail).

Here's a view from Scripture as to what all that can look like.

> *"Thus says the Lord of hosts, 'Consider and call for the mourning women, that they may come; and send for the wailing women, that they may come! Let them make haste and take up a wailing for us, that our eyes may shed tears and our eyelids flow with water.'"*
> ~Jer. 9:17-19

NOTE: I'm not connecting that passage directly to the

PARTICULAR PONDERING(S)

"sowing in tears" concept of Ps. 126. Rather, I'm using it as a biblical example of how lamenting was understood historically during both the Old and New Testament eras.

I'll point out something specifically from the scene in Jer. 9 to help fashion a contextual shape for what I'm addressing. From that text, it is clear that two things are to take place:

There were people (in this case women) who were known in the community to have the gift/ministry of lamentation in their lives. Verse 17 says that they were to be called for—meaning they were known by their reputations.

Their job was to come settle in among those who weren't moved to tears and then to release their own tears in order for there to be a corporate response of lamenting, or lamentation. That role is most clearly not one that is practiced with any degree of interest or regularity among our congregation any longer.

Returning to the Ps. 126 passage, the language used makes it clear that the tears being mentioned are not tears of joy. How do I come up with that conclusion? Because the shouts of joy come after the sowing with tears has taken place. The shouts also come after the harvest has happened as well. The labor(s) of sowing seem to carry with them a burden of sorts. As if the seed being carried and sown might be considered as a weight of responsibility which comes with the sowing process. Think of it as a sort of spiritual sweat equity.

"Nothing worth having comes without some kind of fight. You've got to kick at the darkness 'til it bleeds daylight." (B. Cockburn)

To continue with the text under consideration:

The joy is not contained in the labor of sowing. Rather, it manifests after the labor has been done at the time of harvest. The fruit(s) of the process is when the reveal of joy takes place. When the accounting for the gathered-in sheaves takes place, celebration begins! The benefits come post-labor, not pre-labor. The task at hand can often be labor intensive. Nonetheless, the prize if you will is found when the entire process has been completed.

So, keep these two narratives from Scripture clear and present in your mind:

The harvest is the point of the process, and it is the Lord who is in charge over it.

> *"This means the one who plants is not anybody special, nor the one who waters, for God is the one who brings the supernatural growth. Now, the one who plants and the one who waters are equally important and on the same team, but each will be rewarded for his own work. We are coworkers with God and you are God's cultivated garden, the house he is building.*
> ~1 Cor. 3:7-9 (TPT)

When we are given the opportunity to serve as sowers, our job is singular. We are to sow. The harvesting portion of the process isn't ours to fulfill. That's the work of others in the field. Ultimately it's the work of the One who owns the field(s) and everything in and on them.

> *"He told another story. "God's kingdom is like a farmer who planted good seed in his field. That night, while his hired men were asleep, his enemy sowed thistles all through the wheat*

and slipped away before dawn. When the first green shoots appeared and the grain began to form, the thistles showed up, too. "The farmhands came to the farmer and said, 'Master, that was clean seed you planted, wasn't it? Where did these thistles come from?' "He answered, 'Some enemy did this.' "The farmhands asked, 'Should we weed out the thistles?' "He said, 'No, if you weed the thistles, you'll pull up the wheat, too. Let them grow together until harvest time. Then I'll instruct the harvesters to pull up the thistles and tie them in bundles for the fire, then gather the wheat and put it in the barn.""

~Mt. 13:24-30 (MSG)

"Sow with a view to righteousness, reap in accordance with kindness; break up your fallow ground, for it is time to seek the Lord until He comes to rain righteousness on you."

~Hosea 10:12

A Pondering
CHATTERING(S)

At this very moment as you're reading this, there are more conversations taking place on earth than you can possibly fathom. The tally of such a vast array of verbiage is humanly incalculable. I even wonder if an A. I. program would be capable of totaling up such an accumulation of words. The combined number would most certainly stagger the mind.

At the exact same time, the percentage of discussions taking place based on the subject of the Kingdom of God (what it is / how it was designed to function / and what humanity's response to it should be) would likely be infinitesimal by comparison. That, dear reader, is exactly why humankind's pitifully fallen condition combined with the earth's increasing chaos is taking place. It's not our varied religious beliefs; our political positions; our cultural mores; our moral values (or lack thereof). Nor is it the dysfunction of our manmade structures of education, our personal temporal goals, dreams, and desires, or our collective aspirations. It's distraction from what is to be our 1st Priority! It's our almost total disregard for what the Lord Christ Jesus told us was the Divine will of His Father (our Creator) for all who dwell on earth (past, present,

PARTICULAR PONDERING(S)

and future)—His kingdom come, and His will be done, on earth as it is in heaven. (Mt. 6:10)

What we are witnessing is the ongoing manifestation of everything that works exactly opposite to how the Kingdom of God was designed and intended to function.

Consider this carefully and prayerfully:

> "The Sermon on the Mount has as its context the kingdom of God: "Then He made a tour through the whole of Galilee, teaching in their synagogues, preaching the gospel of the Reign…when He saw the crowds, He went up the hill and sat down, His disciples came up to Him and opening His lips He began to teach them. He said, 'Blessed are—' (Mt. 4:23, 25; 5:1-3, Moffatt). Then follows the Sermon on the Mount which was an extension of the gospel of the Kingdom which He was preaching. In fact the sermon is an expounding of the laws, principles, and attitudes of the kingdom of God…but it was more than a expounding, it was an exposure of His own soul, a photograph of His own inner and outer life and thus an exposure of His life in the kingdom. For He was the Kingdom embodied. This sermon is vascular. Cut it anywhere and it will bleed…it is a life sketch of God, the Son of God, the kingdom of God, and the sons of the kingdom of God…take every item in the sermon and do the opposite of what it inculcates. You will be wrong—dead wrong. Take any item in the sermon and embody it and you will be right—absolutely right."
>
> ~E. Stanley Jones

When I was growing up there was a phrase I'd hear on

occasion. It was intended as a disparaging comment about someone's way of thinking and living.

They're so heavenly minded that they're no earthly good

Now, at the stage I've come to in my own life, I see that statement as being the exact opposite of what it should have been. A better, biblical way of saying it would be,

They're so heavenly minded that the life they live should be considered as a high value asset to the world.

Why am I saying that? For this reason:

"…for where your treasure is, there your heart will be also."
~Mt. 6:21

Consider these passages as they relate to how we live out our 1st Priority:

"So here's what I want you to do, God helping you: Take your everyday, ordinary life—your sleeping, eating, going-to-work, and walking-around life—and place it before God as an offering. Embracing what God does for you is the best thing you can do for him. Don't become so well-adjusted to your culture that you fit into it without even thinking. Instead, fix your attention on God. You'll be changed from the inside out. Readily recognize what he wants from you, and quickly respond to it. Unlike the culture around you, always dragging you down to its level of immaturity, *God brings the best out of you, develops well-formed maturity in you."*
~Rom. 12:1–2 (MSG, emphasis mine)

"Christ's resurrection is your resurrection too. This is why we

are to yearn for all that is above, *for that's where Christ sits enthroned at the place of all power, honor, and authority! Yes, feast on all the treasures of the heavenly realm and fill your thoughts with heavenly realities, and not with the distractions of the natural realm."*

~Col. 3:1–2 (TPT, emphasis mine)

"There's more: God's Word warns us of danger and directs us to hidden treasure. Otherwise how will we find our way? Or know when we play the fool? Clean the slate, God, so we can start the day fresh! Keep me from stupid sins, from thinking I can take over your work; *then I can start this day sun-washed, scrubbed clean of the grime of sin. These are the words in my mouth; these are what I chew on and pray. Accept them when I place them on the morning altar, O God, my Altar-Rock, God, Priest-of-My-Altar."*

~Ps. 19:14 (MSG, emphasis mine)

"So teach us to number our days that we may get a heart of wisdom."

~Ps. 90:12 (ESV)

"But as for me, I trust in You, O Lord, I say, 'You are my God.' My times are in Your hand…"

~Ps. 31;14–15a (ESV)

"…they saw it way off in the distance, waved their greeting, and accepted the fact that they were transients in this world. People who live this way make it plain that they are looking for their true home. If they were homesick for the old country,

they could have gone back any time they wanted. But they were after a far better country than that—heaven country."
~Heb. 11:13-16 (MSG, emphasis mine)

... *"they saw beyond the horizon the fulfillment of their promises and gladly embraced it from afar. They all lived their lives on earth as those who belonged to another realm."*
~Heb. 11:13-16 (TPT, emphasis mine)

"Yet, my brothers, I do not consider myself to have 'arrived', spiritually, nor do I consider myself already perfect. But I keep going on, grasping ever more firmly that purpose for which Christ grasped me. My brothers, I do not consider myself to have fully grasped it even now. But I do concentrate on this: I leave the past behind and with hands outstretched to whatever lies ahead I go straight for the goal—my reward the honor of being called by God in Christ."
~Phil. 3:14-21 (Phillips, emphasis mine)

Jesus Christ, being the most important person who has ever lived on earth, gave a charge to those who were to follow Him. He stated very specifically that it was to be the priority by which we are to live our lives "on earth as it is in heaven". He said, *"seek first the kingdom of God and His righteousness…"*
~Mt. 6:33

Our collective, daily, ongoing, and distractive conversations make it all too clear that the dynamic out-workings of that charge aren't taking place. At least not at the level of being the first and foremost item on humanity's collective to-do list.

PARTICULAR PONDERING(S)

The goal of God's Word, His will, and His ways is given to humankind in many various places throughout the Scriptures. One in specific provides a clearly defined image to work toward:

> *"For the earth will be full of the knowledge of the Lord as the waters cover the sea."*
>
> -Isa. 11:9b

It's not too late to allow the Holy Ghost to help us re-set our personal and corporate priority to reflect what Scripture tells us is to be the main thing considered, and applied to how we live our lives. Start now.

Now hear this:
Song: "Cover The Earth" by Lakewood Church Worship Team—https://www.youtube.com/watch?v=k6xmUji3M6E

A Pondering
JOSEPH'S JOURNEY:

For me, this is one of the most dynamic and fascinating stories in the Bible. The Holy Ghost has used it as a reminder of how life can unravel during difficult times and unexpected circumstances. The sequence of events it reveals serve as powerful and profound lessons in how to deal with life's unexpected drama(s). I have used Joseph's story as a counseling resource too many times to count over the last forty years or so.

Two key considerations take place in the narrative that I'm going to take a look at. The first one is how the story begins based on Joseph's decision to share his dream. The other is to probe what the possible cost(s) can be involved as a prophetic word is progressing to its fulfillment.

There are four specific encounters which take place as the story unfolds. I'll only touch on them briefly. My main focus will be how the story begins, and how it ends. The other touch points that come in between are events which serve to move the process along—they're plot points so to speak. As important as they are to the story, they are only sign posts as the journey unfolds.

NOTE: I'm including the Scriptural narrative because it's worth a re-reading in order to capture the impact of what it says.

PARTICULAR PONDERING(S)

PROCLAIMED PROMISE (Gen. 37:1-12)

Here's how the story begins:

"Now Jacob lived in the land where his father had sojourned, in the land of Canaan. These are the records of the generations of Jacob. Joseph, when seventeen years of age, was pasturing the flock with his brothers while he was still a youth, along with the sons of Bilhah and the sons of Zilpah, his father's wives. And Joseph brought back a bad report about them to their father. Now Israel loved Joseph more than all his sons, because he was the son of his old age; and he made him a varicolored tunic. His brothers saw that their father loved him more than all his brothers; and so they hated him and could not speak to him on friendly terms. Then Joseph had a dream, and when he told it to his brothers, they hated him even more. He said to them, "Please listen to this dream which I have had; for behold, we were binding sheaves in the field, and lo, my sheaf rose up and also stood erect; and behold, your sheaves gathered around and bowed down to my sheaf."

Then his brothers said to him, "Are you actually going to reign over us? Or are you really going to rule over us?" So they hated him even more for his dreams and for his words. Now he had still another dream, and related it to his brothers, and said, "Lo, I have had still another dream; and behold, the sun and the moon and eleven stars were bowing down to me." He related it to his father and to his brothers; and his father rebuked him and said to him, "What is this dream that you have had? Shall I and your mother and your brothers actually come to bow ourselves down before you to the ground?" His brothers were jealous of him, but his father kept the saying in mind."

Here at the beginning we're told that Joseph has a dream. However we're not told at this point where the dream has come from. We only know its origin based on the rest of the story—which at this stage isn't revealed. So, Joseph doesn't mention how he thinks it has been imparted. We're only told what he did with it, which was to share it with his family.

Personally I think Joseph lacked wisdom by sharing what he did, the way he did. Since there's no mention of where the dream came from, and no direction given to him by Jehovah to share it, I wonder what his motivation was to even bring it up at all.

Let me pose a couple of questions here: What would your reaction be if you and your family were to be presented with such a story from your brother? In other words, how would you choose to respond to what seemed like a pretentious and condescending statement?

It seems to me that Joseph could have kept his vision to himself. In a sense it appears that his comments brought on what happened next.

PIT PLIGHT (Gen. 37:12-36)

"Then his brothers went to pasture their father's flock in Shechem. Israel said to Joseph, "Are not your brothers pasturing the flock in Shechem? Come, and I will send you to them." And he said to him, I will go." Then he said to him, "Go now and see about the welfare of your brothers and the welfare of the flock, and bring word back to me." So he sent

PARTICULAR PONDERING(S)

him from the valley of Hebron, and he came to Shechem. A man found him, and behold, he was wandering in the field; and the man asked him, "What are you looking for?" He said, "I am looking for my brothers; please tell me where they are pasturing the flock." Then the man said, "They have moved from here; for I heard them say, 'Let us go to Dothan.'" So Joseph went after his brothers and found them at Dothan. When they saw him from a distance and before he came close to them, they plotted against him to put him to death. They said to one another, "Here comes this dreamer! Now then, come and let us kill him and throw him into one of the pits; and we will say, 'A wild beast devoured him.' Then let us see what will become of his dreams!" But Reuben heard this and rescued him out of their hands and said, "Let us not take his life." Reuben further said to them, "Shed no blood. Throw him into this pit that is in the wilderness, but do not lay hands on him"—that he might rescue him out of their hands, to restore him to his father. So it came about, when Joseph reached his brothers, that they stripped Joseph of his tunic, the varicolored tunic that was on him; and they took him and threw him into the pit. Now the pit was empty, without any water in it."

Up to this point in the story there has been no mention of Jehovah being involved in anything that has taken place. Joseph shared his revelation, and his family responded to it out of their carnal-fleshly-human-emotions. Although their response was clearly inappropriate and outrageous, it was nonetheless understandable. Still today, there are people in places around the world where such things still take place. Such is the case with humankind's fallen/sinful condition. Our so-called personal values, social mores, and cultural ethics constantly continue to violate God's Biblically-based principles and precepts.

From here the dynamics of the story begin to intensify: Continued from Gen. 37:25-)

> *"Then they sat down to eat a meal. And as they raised their eyes and looked, behold, a caravan of Ishmaelites was coming from Gilead, with their camels bearing aromatic gum and balm and myrrh, on their way to bring them down to Egypt. Judah said to his brothers, "What profit is it for us to kill our brother and cover up his blood? Come and let us sell him to the Ishmaelites and not lay our hands on him, for he is our brother, our own flesh." And his brothers listened to him. Then some Midianite traders passed by, so they pulled him up and lifted Joseph out of the pit, and sold him to the Ishmaelites for twenty shekels of silver. Thus they brought Joseph into Egypt. Now Reuben returned to the pit, and behold, Joseph was not in the pit; so he tore his garments. He returned to his brothers and said, "The boy is not there; as for me, where am I to go?" So they took Joseph's tunic, and slaughtered a male goat and dipped the tunic in the blood; and they sent the varicolored tunic and brought it to their father and said, "We found this; please examine it to see whether it is your son's tunic or not." Then he examined it and said, "It is my son's tunic. A wild beast has devoured him; Joseph has surely been torn to pieces!" So Jacob tore his clothes, and put sackcloth on his loins and mourned for his son many days. Then all his sons and all his daughters arose to comfort him, but he refused to be comforted. And he said, "Surely I will go down to Sheol in mourning for my son." So*

his father wept for him. Meanwhile, the Midianites sold him in Egypt to Potiphar, Pharaoh's officer, the captain of the bodyguard."

PROBLEMS AT POTIPHER'S PLACE (Gen. 39:1-18)

"Now Joseph had been taken down to Egypt; and Potiphar, an Egyptian officer of Pharaoh, the captain of the bodyguard, bought him from the Ishmaelites, who had taken him down there. The Lord was with Joseph, so he became a successful man. And he was in the house of his master, the Egyptian. Now his master saw that the Lord was with him and how the Lord caused all that he did to prosper in his hand. So Joseph found favor in his sight and became his personal servant; and he made him overseer over his house, and all that he owned he put in his charge. It came about that from the time he made him overseer in his house and over all that he owned, the Lord blessed the Egyptian's house on account of Joseph; thus the Lord's blessing was upon all that he owned, in the house and in the field. So he left everything he owned in Joseph's charge; and with him there he did not concern himself with anything except the food which he ate. Now Joseph was handsome in form and appearance. It came about after these events that his master's wife looked with desire at Joseph, and she said, "Lie with me." But he refused and said to his master's wife, "Behold, with me here, my master does not concern himself with anything in the house, and he has put all that he owns in my charge. There is no one greater in this house than I, and he has withheld nothing from me except you, because you are his wife. How then could I do this great evil and sin against God?" As she spoke to Joseph

day after day, he did not listen to her to lie beside her or be with her. Now it happened one day that he went into the house to do his work, and none of the men of the household was there inside. She caught him by his garment, saying, "Lie with me!" And he left his garment in her hand and fled, and went outside. When she saw that he had left his garment in her hand and had fled outside, she called to the men of her household and said to them, "See, he has brought in a Hebrew to us to make sport of us; he came in to me to lie with me, and I screamed. When he heard that I raised my voice and screamed, he left his garment beside me and fled and went outside." So she left his garment beside her until his master came home. Then she spoke to him with these words, "The Hebrew slave, whom you brought to us, came in to me to make sport of me; and as I raised my voice and screamed, he left his garment beside me and fled outside."

Things go from bad to worse. The first two plot points have now passed. There is an interesting development unfolding in regards to an aspect of Joseph's character. From the pit to the issue at Potipher's house, we've not a word of any grumbling or complaining. In light of what's to follow, that's a trait worth taking note of.

From here the scene becomes much more desperate and restrictive. The unraveling in Joseph's life becomes seemingly more hopeless.

PRISON (Gen. 39:19-23)

"Now when his master heard the words of his wife, which she spoke to him, saying, "This is what your slave did to me," his

> *anger burned. So Joseph's master took him and put him into the jail, the place where the king's prisoners were confined; and he was there in the jail. But the Lord was with Joseph and extended kindness to him, and gave him favor in the sight of the chief jailer. The chief jailer committed to Joseph's charge all the prisoners who were in the jail; so that whatever was done there, he was responsible for it. The chief jailer did not supervise anything under Joseph's charge because the Lord was with him; and whatever he did, the Lord made to prosper."*

The story now begins to focus in on a detail which up to this point had not even been mentioned. We're told, *"the LORD was with him; and whatever he did, the LORD made to prosper."* That statement sheds an entirely new light on what has been taking place. The inner-play of the characters, the plot lines, and the pending resolution lie just beyond us as the journey unfolds.

PLACEMENT PROCESSING (Gen. 40)

> *"Then it came about after these things, the cupbearer and the baker for the king of Egypt offended their lord, the king of Egypt. Pharaoh was furious with his two officials, the chief cupbearer and the chief baker. So he put them in confinement in the house of the captain of the bodyguard, in the jail, the same place where Joseph was imprisoned. The captain of the bodyguard put Joseph in charge of them, and he took care of them; and they were in confinement for some time. Then the cupbearer and the baker for the king of Egypt, who were confined in jail, both had a dream the same night, each man with his own dream and each dream with its own interpretation. When Joseph came to them in the morning and observed*

them, behold, they were dejected. He asked Pharaoh's officials who were with him in confinement in his master's house, "Why are your faces so sad today?" Then they said to him, "We have had a dream and there is no one to interpret it." Then Joseph said to them, "Do not interpretations belong to God? Tell it to me, please." So the chief cupbearer told his dream to Joseph, and said to him, "In my dream, behold, there was a vine in front of me; and on the vine were three branches. And as it was budding, its blossoms came out, and its clusters produced ripe grapes. Now Pharaoh's cup was in my hand; so I took the grapes and squeezed them into Pharaoh's cup, and I put the cup into Pharaoh's hand." Then Joseph said to him, "This is the interpretation of it: the three branches are three days; within three more days Pharaoh will lift up your head and restore you to your office; and you will put Pharaoh's cup into his hand according to your former custom when you were his cupbearer. Only keep me in mind when it goes well with you, and please do me a kindness by mentioning me to Pharaoh and get me out of this house. For I was in fact kidnapped from the land of the Hebrews, and even here I have done nothing that they should have put me into the dungeon." When the chief baker saw that he had interpreted favorably, he said to Joseph, "I also saw in my dream, and behold, there were three baskets of white bread on my head; and in the top basket there were some of all sorts of baked food for Pharaoh, and the birds were eating them out of the basket on my head." Then Joseph answered and said, "This is its interpretation: the three baskets are three days; within three more days Pharaoh will lift up your head from you and will hang you on a tree, and the birds will eat your flesh off you." Thus it came about on the third day, which was Pharaoh's birthday, that he made a feast for all his servants; and he lifted up the head of the chief cupbearer and the head of the chief baker among his servants. He restored the chief cupbearer to his office, and he put the cup into Pharaoh's hand; but he hanged the chief baker, just as Joseph had interpreted to them. Yet the chief cupbearer did not remember Joseph, but forgot him."

PALACE (Gen. 41-47)

The pathway from the prison to the palace is a lengthy one in terms of Scriptural content. I encourage you to read it on your own in order to get the entire story. If/When you do, you'll arrive at the destination—well, almost. There's one more passage for consideration which will help you to really understand the journey from beginning to end.

RIGHT PLACE, RIGHT TIME (Ps. 105:16-24)

"And He called for a famine upon the land; He broke the whole staff of bread.

He sent a man before them, Joseph, who was sold as a slave. They afflicted his feet with fetters, He himself was laid in irons; until the time that his word came to pass, the word of the Lord tested him. The king sent and released him, the ruler of peoples, and set him free. He made him lord of his house and ruler over all his possessions, to imprison his princes at will, that he might teach his elders wisdom. Israel also came into Egypt; thus Jacob sojourned in the land of Ham. And He caused His people to be very fruitful, and made them stronger than their adversaries."

Herein lies the heart of the entire sojourn. In this passage we are told exactly (and specifically) why, how, and when everything we've been considering took place. Why? In order for Jehovah's word to come to pass. What word would that be? The exact word that was given to Joseph that he shared with his brothers. How? By Jehovah testing Joseph with the word he'd been given before his journey even began. When? Prior to the famine which ultimately impacted an entire nation. Which in turn set the stage for Joseph to take up residence in the palace. From his position as second in command under Pharaoh, he was then able to set up the means for his family to enter the land of Goshen. It was there, after some four hundred years of captivity that Moses would be born, grow up, and provide the leadership necessary to guide God's people to deliverance and freedom from the bondage of slavery.

A truly remarkable story indeed!

A Pondering

KINGDOM CITIZENSHIP vs. NATIONALIZED CHRISTIANITY

Before I develop this narrative any further, I'll make four brief statements. That way if you feel your blood pressure rising as you're reading them you can simply back away.

The Kingdom of God (Christ's kingdom) is not of this world. He said so Himself (Jn. 18:36) It is eternal, not temporal.

There are no national flags behind or around the throne of God. (Deut. 5:7) NOTE: Most translations say *"no other gods before Me."* However the NASB says, *"no other gods besides Me."* I much prefer that concept. It seems considerable broader in what it encompasses.

The nation we were born into here on earth has absolutely nothing to do with the eternal citizenship of a follower of Christ (1 Pet. 2:9). Each component (category) of that passage is past tense. Meaning that as followers of Christ we are already included in each one. We don't have to earn them, grow into them, or perfect them. They came with our redemption package so to speak.

"The government shall be upon His *shoulders"*
~Isa. 9:6, emphasis mine

I'll factor in the following definitions in order to help focus in on what I'm addressing:

KINGDOM (from the KJV): n.
1. The territory or country subject to a king; an undivided territory under the dominion of a king or monarch.
2. The inhabitants or population subject to a king.
3. In natural history, a division; as the animal, vegetable and mineral kingdoms.
4. A region; a tract; the place where anything prevails and holds sway; as the watery kingdom.
5. In Scripture, the government or universal dominion of God. 1 Chron. 29. Ps.1 45.
6. The power of supreme administration. 1 Sam. 18.
7. A princely nation or state: "Ye shall be unto me a kingdom of priests." Ex. 19.
8. Heaven. Mt. 26.
9. State of glory in heaven. Mt. 5.
10. The reign of the Messiah. Mt. 3.
11. Government; rule; supreme administration.
(From Webster's) NOUN
a country, state, or territory ruled by a king or queen: "the Kingdom of the Netherlands"
synonyms:
realm · domain · dominion · country · land · nation · state · sovereign state ·
a realm associated with or regarded as being under the control of a particular person or thing: "the kingdom of dreams"
synonyms:
domain · province · realm · sphere · sphere/field of influence · the spiritual reign or authority of God.

the rule of God or Christ in a future age.

each of the three traditional divisions (animal, vegetable, and mineral) in which natural objects have conventionally been classified.

CITIZENSHIP (from Scripture)
1. The native of a city, or an inhabitant who enjoys the freedom and privileges of the city in which he resides; the freeman of a city, as distinguished from a foreigner, or one not entitled to its franchises.
2. A townsman; a man of trade; not a gentleman.
3. An inhabitant; a dweller in any city, town or place.
4. In a general sense, a native or permanent resident in a city or country.

CITIZEN: adj. Having the qualities of a citizen.
(From Webster's) NOUN: The position or status of being a citizen of a particular country.

NATIONALISM (From Webster's): NOUN

Identification with one's own nation and support for its interests, especially to the exclusion or detriment of the interests of other nations. Advocacy of or support for the political independence of a particular nation or people.

CHRISTIANITY (from Scripture): The name given by the Greeks or Romans, probably in reproach, to the followers of Jesus. It was first used at Antioch. The names by which the disciples were known among themselves were "brethren," "the faithful," "elect," "saints," "believers." But as distinguishing them from the multitude without, the name "Christian" came into use, and was universally accepted. This name occurs but three times in the New Testament (Acts 11:26 ; 26:28 ; 1 Pet. 4:16).

(From Webster's)

The religion based on the person and teachings of Jesus of Nazareth, or its beliefs and practices. Christian quality or character.

POLITICS:

1. The activities associated with the governance of a country or other area, especially the debate or conflict among individuals or parties having or hoping to achieve power.

2. The activities of governments concerning the political relations between countries.

3. The academic study of government and the stated activities within an organization that are aimed at improving someone's status or position and are typically considered to be devious or divisive.

4. A particular set of political beliefs or principles.

5. The assumptions or principles relating to or inherent in a sphere, theory, or thing, especially when concerned with power and status in a society.

I'll use but one verse to establish a foundation to build this narrative upon.

"The government shall be upon His shoulders."

~Isa. 9:6

How those who are not born again accept, relate, or conform

to that verse is of little concern to me as I draft this out. My thoughts are directed solely to those who are followers of Christ, citizens of heaven, God's loyal and obedient subjects, His servants, His *worshipers. All those who are "in Christ Jesus" (Col. 3:1-3) have already been transferred into the Kingdom of God.

*Worship is obedient service manifesting through self-sacrifice.

"As you live this new life, we pray that you will be strengthened from God's boundless resources, so that you will find yourselves able to pass through any experience and endure it with courage. You will even be able to thank God in the midst of pain and distress because you are privileged to share the lot of those who are living in the light. For we must never forget that he rescued us from the power of darkness, and re-established us in the kingdom of his beloved Son, that is, in the kingdom of light. For it is by his Son alone that we have been redeemed and have had our sins forgiven."
~Col. 1:13 (Phillips)

NOTE: That passage is past tense as is 1 Pet. 2:9. Meaning everything it states has already come to pass. It is therefore a pro-active-dynamic to be lived in and lived out of by born again believers.

Those of us who are branded/sealed (Eph. 4:30) as Christians have a personal and collective scriptural charge (responsibility) to live our lives here on earth while at the same time functioning as citizens of an eternal kingdom, which is not part of any earthly kingdom(s) as such. Based on the level of sensitivity surrounding the subject of politics, I'd prefer not to deal with this topic at all. Just broaching it often leads to *fightin' words*.

Nonetheless I have come to a place where I am convinced that the subject must be considered as foundational as it relates to one's spiritual evolution and temporal nationalistic citizenship. Here's why: Government has been an issue on earth ever since humankind walked out of The Garden. You see, there is an aspect to living on the planet which we humans can't seem to get sorted out. It is this:

We resist/rebel against anyone or anything which attempts to have charge or take charge of our lives. The enemy of our souls (Satan) had the exact same problem. I'll address that later.

We do that individually as a person as well as collectively as a people group (or nation). Without wandering out too far into such a theological minefield, I'll cautiously attempt to point out a pathway for you to walk with me from this side to the other, toward a safer biblically-based place to stand regarding our political positioning, pundit posturing(s), and personal preferences.

Perhaps the best/simplest examples of Biblically historical power struggle is found in the story of the Tower of Babel.

> *"Now the whole earth used the same language and the same words. It came about as they journeyed east, that they found a plain in the land of Shinar and settled there.*
>
> *They said to one another, "Come, let us make bricks and burn them thoroughly." And they used brick for stone, and they used tar for mortar. They said, "Come, let us build for ourselves a city, and a tower whose top will reach into heaven, and let us make for ourselves a name, otherwise we will be scattered abroad over the face of the whole earth." The Lord came down to see the city and the tower which the sons of men had built.*

PARTICULAR PONDERING(S)

> *The Lord said, "Behold, they are one people, and they all have the same language. And this is what they began to do, and now nothing which they purpose to do will be impossible for them. Come, let Us go down and there confuse their language, so that they will not understand one another's speech."*
>
> *So the Lord scattered them abroad from there over the face of the whole earth; and they stopped building the city. Therefore its name was called Babel, because there the Lord confused the language of the whole earth; and from there the Lord scattered them abroad over the face of the whole earth."*
>
> ~Gen. 11:1-9

That is a truly amazing story to ponder. To begin with, it is (or may be) the only place in Scripture where we find the three persons of the Trinity conversing with themselves. The Lord makes an observational statement to the other two parties (v.6). Then He suggests to them that *they* should go down to earth and shake things up. The reason is clearly stated in v.6 which says, *"this is what they began to do, and now nothing which they purpose to do will be impossible for them."* In other words, the Creator Himself understands that the gift of creativity which had been imparted directly into the DNA of humanity by His Divine hand (See Gen. 1:1) when left unchecked—or ungoverned—can accomplish *anything!* That's what the text says.

The purposed intentions of the people in this story are twofold:

Let us make for ourselves a city—*their* city

Let us make a name for ourselves

As I read this passage I see the roots of two key negative/fallen human attributes manifesting. Firstly, a move toward self-aggrandizement (creating a self-centered, self-powered, self-driven, destiny). Secondly, a move toward self-governance—based on ego and personal achievement. If those things aren't key components in the political process, I don't know what is.

All strivings for power, control, fame, and recognition has at its base a political aspect. As such, moving in that direction and in those circles tends to separate those involved from this Scriptural truth:

All power and authority belong to God in Christ.

"Then Jesus came close to them and said, 'All the authority of the universe has been given to me.'"
~Mt. 28:18 (TPT)

My intention here isn't to challenge, correct, or condescend toward anyone's personal political beliefs. Such matters are not mine to involve myself with directly (see Ps. 131). How people feel about politicians, party-lines, and government(s) in specific isn't my concern. However, as a follower of Christ, it seems to me that the political dynamics of kingdom citizenship should—at the very least—be given some serious consideration as to what Jesus said was to be the 1st priority of His followers (Mt. 6:33).

Seeking the Kingdom of God first and foremost is a charge fashioned and framed around who (or what) is to be considered as Sovereign in the lives of Christians. I am merely attempting to convey what I understand to be a Biblically-based perspective regarding how believers are to view temporal government(s), politics, and politicians. This article is meant to draw a comparison between how such things are to be evaluated and addressed from two separate viewpoints. One is temporal, earth-based, and established within the framework of earth-time. The other is eternal, formed outside of time (with no beginning, middle, or end). One is man-made, and limited to usage here on this planet. The other is God-designed, without limits, and intended to function throughout eternity. One changes based on shifts in culture, historical transitions, and the process of life and death. The other never changes—having only One Sovereign Ruler over the subjects/citizens of a heavenly kingdom. Scripturally speaking, that's known as the Kingdom of God.

Here's another story from Biblical history that presents a picture of how spiritual life is impacted by politics:

> *"...while Joshua was there near Jericho: He looked up and saw right in front of him a man standing, holding his drawn sword. Joshua stepped up to him and said, 'Whose side are you on—ours or our enemies?' He said, 'Neither. I'm commander of God's army.'"*
>
> ~Josh.5:13–14 (MSG)

If you were to hold that verse up and let light refract through it, you might see an aspect of the politics of opposing sides reflected in the interchange. Joshua is concerned about taking sides—an earthbound perspective. He is after all earthbound in his concerns. While at the same time the angel is not from around here. He was sent from eternity, representing God's government and God's way of discharging His Divine authority. So, his response is neither on behalf of one side, nor the other. His statement validates the positional directive which came from the throne of God—the seat of eternal governance.

To repeat: I'm not taking sides or trying to build a case (pro or con) for the political processes of earthly government(s). That's not anywhere near my intention; I'm trying to clarify/

inform/remind anyone who's reading this that the who's and how's of any and all forms of earth-based government(s) have no lasting/eternal value in terms of the Kingdom of God and those who occupy it. When any form of man-made/man-led government is allowed to become so inner-linked into how the governance of Jehovah is designed to function, there is a grave danger of the temporal forms supplanting the eternal one.

The title of this essay is, "KINGDOM CITIZENSHIP vs. NATIONALIZED CHRISTIANITY." I'm attempting to draw a comparison between the two in order to point out the distinctions which should exist—but increasingly don't. At least not as I see such distinctions in these daze we're living in.

Another example from Scripture. This happened when the political leader of the day (Herod) took steps to remove his competition:

"Now after Jesus was born in Bethlehem of Judea in the days of Herod the king, behold, wise men from the east came to Jerusalem, saying,

"Where is he who has been born king of the Jews? For we saw his star when it rose and have come to worship him."

When Herod the king heard this, he was troubled, and all Jerusalem with him; and assembling all the chief priests and scribes of the people, he inquired of them where the Christ was to be born.

They told him, "In Bethlehem of Judea, for so it is written by the prophet: "'And you, O Bethlehem, in the land of Judah, are by no means least among the rulers of Judah; for from you shall come a ruler who will shepherd my people Israel.'"

~Mt. 2:1-06

PARTICULAR PONDERING(S)

Herod is about to search for the child, to destroy him. *As was then, so is now*—politics can get very ugly indeed.

Out of many more Scriptural narratives, there's one more worth pondering:

The most dangerous counter-cultural-terrorist in opposition to the Kingdom of God is Satan. His pit-fall (pun intended) was based solely on his prideful desire for political dominance. He had power and control issues. His intent was to rule the universe. Pride was at the very heart of his downfall.

"Lift yourself up with pride and you will soon be brought low..."
~Pro. 29:23a (TPT)

"But you said in your heart, 'I will ascend to heaven; I will raise my throne above the stars of God, and I will sit on the mount of assembly in the recesses of the north. 'I will ascend above the heights of the clouds; I will make myself like the Most High.'
~Isa. 14:13–14

Consider 1 Pet. 5:6 which provides us a clear and concise explanation of how pride can lead to all sorts of chaos, personal and corporate drama, and a totally misdirected comprehension of what it means to serve in obedience, yielded to a Sovereign King as a loyal citizen in His kingdom.

"If you bow low in God's awesome presence, he will eventually exalt you as you leave the timing in his hands."
~1 Pet. 5:6 (TPT)

It's our job to humble ourselves. It's God's job to exalt us (on His terms and in His timing). If we insist on doing His job, He has no choice but to do ours.

God's either in charge or He's not. He's either sovereign or He's not. He's either the One True God over all His creation or He's not. The government is either on His shoulders or it's not. See a pattern here?

BROKEN ONES
(Ps. 51:17)

When you bow down, way down
You may find a place where few have gone
And if you stay down, stay way down
You may see some things that few are shown

If you'll humble yourself under His mighty hand
He will lift you up, and steady you to stand

He will embrace the broken ones…

When you give up, really give up
You can find your place of sweet release
And if you'll give up, completely give up
God will flood your heart with perfect peace

If you'll humble yourself under His mighty hand
He will lift you up, and steady you to stand

He will embrace the broken ones…

(W. Berry / See & Say Songs, BMI)

PARTICULAR PONDERING(S)

I've not meaning to mess with anyone's political preferences as such, nor their voting history. How one's affiliations and loyalties are established concerning their homeland is for the most part none of my business or my concern. However, here in America, how one sorts through subjects like *patriotism, national pride, and service-to-country is between them and their own conscious, I suppose. (See Heb. 11:14.) I personally don't see a way for followers of Christ to reconcile the elevation of nationalistic pride (mind-set or heart-set) above that of their kingdom birthright without creating theological inconsistency, corporate disunity, unclarified testimony, and a general weakening of the biblically-based principles, precepts, and core values. I am aware that may just be me stating my personal point of view. That being said, this is, after all, a book based on my own pondering(s) of things such as this. So, there ya go.

> *Patriotism or national pride is the feeling of love, devotion and sense of attachment to a homeland and alliance with other citizens who share the same sentiment. This attachment can be a combination of many different feelings relating to one's own homeland, including ethnic, cultural, political or historical aspects. It encompasses a set of concepts closely related to nationalism.
> ~Wikipedia

A disclaimer (of a sort): My concern isn't in regards to the structure of temporal government(s) or the process of politics as such. I am well aware of what Scripture has to say about temporal leadership and the structures they operate from.

"Be a good citizen. All governments are under God. Insofar as

there is peace and order, it's God's order. So live responsibly as a citizen. If you're irresponsible to the state, then you're irresponsible with God, and God will hold you responsible. Duly constituted authorities are only a threat if you're trying to get by with something. Decent citizens should have nothing to fear. Do you want to be on good terms with the government? Be a responsible citizen and you'll get on just fine, the government working to your advantage. But if you're breaking the rules right and left, watch out. The police aren't there just to be admired in their uniforms. God also has an interest in keeping order, and he uses them to do it. That's why you must live responsibly—not just to avoid punishment but also because it's the right way to live."

~Rom. 13:1-5 (MSG)

"Remind people to respect their governmental leaders on every level as law-abiding citizens and to be ready to fulfill their civic duty. And remind them to never tear down anyone with their words or quarrel, but instead be considerate, humble, and courteous to everyone."

~Titus 3:1–2 (TPT)

"In order to honor the Lord, you must respect and defer to the authority of every human institution, whether it be the highest ruler or the governors he puts in place to punish lawbreakers and to praise those who do what's right.

For it is God's will for you to silence the ignorance of foolish people by doing what is right. As God's loving servants, you should live in complete freedom, but never use your freedom as a cover-up for evil. Recognize the value of every person and continually show love to every believer. Live your lives

PARTICULAR PONDERING(S)

with great reverence and in holy awe of God. Honor your rulers. Those who are servants, submit to the authority of those who are your masters—not only to those who are kind and gentle but even to those who are hard and difficult. You find God's favor by deciding to please God even when you endure hardships because of unjust suffering. For what merit is it to endure mistreatment for wrongdoing? Yet if you are mistreated when you do what is right, and you faithfully endure it, this is commendable before God. In fact, you were called to live this way, because Christ also suffered in your place, leaving you his example for you to follow. He never sinned and he never spoke deceitfully. When he was verbally abused, he did not return with an insult; when he suffered, he would not threaten retaliation. Jesus faithfully entrusted himself into the hands of God, who judges righteously.

He himself carried our sins in his body on the cross so that we would be dead to sin and live for righteousness. Our instant healing flowed from his wounding.

You were like sheep that continually wandered away but now you have returned to the true Shepherd of your lives—the kind Guardian who lovingly watches over your souls."

1 Pet. 2:13-25 (TPT)

My real concern, the one that's currently breaking my heart, is that so many followers of Christ are living at variance with one another based on how they are misunderstanding temporal-earth-bound-governance and the politics which flow from it. It is sad, so sad, to know that believers who will live together eternally in the glorious afterlife—with the Father, Son, Holy Ghost, and a myriad of all those who have been "accepted into the beloved" (Eph. 1:6)—can't find unity amid diversity here on earth in such matters. As Christians, the so-called left and right should be finding biblically appropriate ways of coming to terms with exactly Whose government they are submitted to and living under. Yes, we are called to yield to and obey the laws of the land we're in. But, there is a high level of submission and service to which God's Word calls us. When we allow any person, place, or thing to override the command given in Deut. 5:7, the results are tragic on a personal as well as a collective/corporate level.

You shall have no other gods before (or besides) Me."
-Deut. 5:7

The politics of the Kingdom of God is the system His people are to represent here on earth as it is in heaven (Mt. 6:10). Those who have been transferred from darkness into light (Col. 1:13) are to live in and out of 1 Pet. 2:9. Otherwise, our ability to carry out the "ministry of reconciliation" (our job description) as "ambassadors for Christ" (our job title) simply isn't possible to fulfill with any degree of honesty, integrity, and authenticity. (See 2 Cor. 5:18-21). The reason we're saved isn't to get to heaven. That's a by-product of redemption. If that were the case, once we've received salvation, we'd have gone directly to heaven. Since we're still here on earth, there must be a reason. There is. It's presented clearly and distinctly in 2 Cor. 5:18-21. Putting what it says we are to do into daily, ongoing practice is why I've written the article.

In closing, think this through:

"Don't hoard treasure down here where it gets eaten by moths and corroded by rust or—worse!—stolen by burglars.

PARTICULAR PONDERING(S)

Stockpile treasure in heaven, where it's safe from moth and rust and burglars. It's obvious, isn't it? The place where your treasure is, is the place you will most want to be, and end up being."

~Mt. 6:21 (MSG)

"Thy kingdom come, Thy will be done, on earth as it is in heaven."

~Mt. 6:10

Here's a somewhat lighter POV…

GLENDALE, CA—A man was rushed to the hospital yesterday after encountering a slightly different viewpoint than his own.

Shortly before 12:30 p.m., Glendale PD officers responded to a 911 call at the Java Lounge Coffee House in the 900 block of North Emerson Road. They found a person who had collapsed in shock and went to the station for help. Witnesses say the man was having a casual conversation about politics with another patron when the minutely opposing viewpoint was expressed.

"They were both Democrats, Bernie supporters," said Janice Hughson, a barista at the Java Lounge. "Then the guy he was talking to said he had some issues with abortion and thinks there should at least be a few limitations put on the practice. That's when the man seized up and began foaming at the mouth. It was terrible."

Four other bystanders were also emotionally injured by the moderately divergent opinion but were not hospitalized.

The man is being kept stable on ideology support at St. Francis medical center, surrounded by friends and family who agree with him 100% on every single issue.

The man who suggested the slightly differing opinion fled the scene. Anyone with information is asked to alert the authorities.

~babylonebee.com

"Battle lines being drawn, nobody's right, if everybody's wrong."
S. Stills

Two resources for consideration:
The Most Important Person On Earth by Myles Munroe
The Way of the Dragon or the Way of the Lamb: Searching for Jesus' Path of Power in a Church that Has Abandoned It by Jamin Goggin and Kyle Strobel

A Pondering
PONDERING TRUST

> *"Trust God from the bottom of your heart; don't try to figure out everything on your own. Listen for God's voice in everything you do, everywhere you go; He's the one who will keep you on track."*
>
> ~Pro. 3:5–6 (MSG)

Learning to live trusting in the Lord is so very important. Trust is not faith, but they spend a lot of time together. They are Biblical cohorts of a sort. Faith has a much harder time of staying vital, strong and active without having trust nearby. In a sense, trust makes space for faith to live in. If trust takes up residence in a life, it'll bring faith along too. Then, when they're together, faith can began to flow freely out of hope (Heb. 11:1). In turn, the ongoing presence of hope will be generated by appropriating grace (2 Thess. 2:16). And grace will renew itself as it's appropriated directly from the throne of grace (Heb. 4:16).

Think of it this way: Grace + Hope = Faith (with Trust as a companion).

Redemptive Components
THE PROCESS OF CONSECRATION

To me, this passage is one of the most important and meaningful in the entire Bible (especially v.17). I'm sharing it in four translations just so you can wrap yourself in the light that it sheds forth.

Side note: Col. 3:17 is my "life verse."

"Let the peace of Christ keep you in tune with each other, in step with each other. None of this going off and doing your own thing. And cultivate thankfulness. Let the Word of Christ—the Message—have the run of the house. Give it plenty of room in your lives. Instruct and direct one another using good common sense. And sing, sing your hearts out to God! Let every detail in your lives—words, actions, whatever—be done in the name of the Master, Jesus, thanking God the Father every step of the way."

~Col. 3:17 (MSG, emphasis mine)

"Let your heart be always guided by the peace of the Anointed One, who called you to peace as part of his one body. And always be thankful. Let the word of Christ live in you

richly, flooding you with all wisdom. Apply the Scriptures as you teach and instruct one another with the Psalms, and with festive praises, and with prophetic songs given to you spontaneously by the Spirit, so sing to God with all your hearts! Let every activity of your lives and every word that comes from your lips be drenched with the beauty of our Lord Jesus, the Anointed One. And bring your constant praise to God the Father because of what Christ has done for you!"

~Col. 3:15-17 (TPT, emphasis mine)

"*Let the peace of Christ rule in your hearts, remembering that as members of the same body you are called to live in harmony, and never forget to be thankful for what God has done for you. Let Christ's teaching live in your hearts, making you rich in the true wisdom. Teach and help one another along the right road with your psalms and hymns and Christian songs, singing God's praises with joyful hearts.* And whatever you may have to do, do everything in the name of the Lord Jesus, thanking God the Father through him."

~Col. 3:15-17 (Phillips, emphasis mine)

"*And let the peace of Christ rule in your hearts, to which indeed you were called in one body. And be thankful. Let the word of Christ dwell in you richly, teaching and admonishing one another in all wisdom, singing psalms and hymns and spiritual songs, with thankfulness in your hearts to God.* And whatever you do, in word or deed, do everything in the name of the Lord Jesus, giving thanks to God the Father through him."

~Col. 3:15-17 (ESV, emphasis mine)

The text tells us to give free reign to the peace of Christ in our lives as His followers. That's because we've been called (appointed) to do so. It also says that thanksgiving should be a pro-active condition in which we live. Further, it directs us to allow the Word of God to have permanent residence in us, which can enable us to teach and admonish one another in wisdom while cultivating the gift of music (in psalms, hymns, and spiritual songs). Each of those aspects of spirituality are deserving of much consideration and application. Then the passage closes by stating one of the most profound Biblical directives in Scripture:

"Whatever you do in word or deed, do all in the name of the Lord Jesus, giving thanks through Him to God the Father."
~Col. 3:17

The charge given there is (as I take it) directly linkable to the principle of biblical consecration. That's the focus of what I'm going to address here.

To begin, this is my working definition for *consecration:* Consecration is the setting apart of any person, place, or thing for acts of holy service.

Without commitment to the principle and practice of consecration, it's impossible to fully implement what Col. 3:17 says we are to do as believers. Here's what I mean by making that statement:

For without first being willing to live a lifestyle which is based on accomplishing acts of holy service, it is impossible to do so. Put simply, surrendering your life to Christ is at its basic level an act of consecration in and of itself. However you prayed your first prayer of confession and repentance, regardless of whether you knew it or not, you were performing your first formative act in the process of consecrating your life to Kingdom service. You were asking the Lord to take your life and set it apart for His service in any way He wanted that to take place. And that is, in fact, consecration. By doing so, you entered into a process which is meant to carry you along the "highway of holiness" (Isa. 35:8a (KJV) which leads all the way up to Zion.

"How enriched are they who find their strength in the Lord; within their hearts are the highways of holiness! Even when their paths wind through the dark valley of tears, they dig deep to find a pleasant pool where others find only pain. He gives to them a brook of blessing filled from the rain of an outpouring. They grow stronger and stronger with every step forward, and the God of all gods will appear before them in Zion."

~Ps. 84:5-7 (TPT)

The so-called Sinner's Prayer is therefore an act of consecration regardless of what words are used or whether or not a full understanding was taking place at the moment. Giving one's life to God, through Christ Jesus, prompted and enabled by the Holy Ghost is without a doubt a consecrated act. However, the original act only begins the process. In other words, the act provides an entrance on to the pathway that followers of Christ are called to walk along till they die or till Jesus returns for His own. At least that's how I understand the principle and practice was designed to function.

Having said all that, I'm going to unpack how I see the process of consecration taking place using some key scriptural examples. In order to do that, I need to clarify a language issue that can be confusing without some clear and concise consideration:

In the KJV (and some other translations), the word *consecration* is presented as being interchangeable with the word *sanctification*. That is misleading as I understand those two terms. As I've already mentioned, consecration begins (or requires) a setting apart. That's our job. In other words, the process is one we have to initiate ourselves. Sanctification is—according to Scripture—the work of the Holy Ghost on our behalf. (See 1 Thess. 4:3 / 1 Pet. 1:2 / Rom. 15:16 / Jude 1)

Here's perhaps the best example from the Word to explain what I'm saying:

"And Joshua said unto the people, "Sanctify yourselves: for tomorrow the Lord will do wonders among you.""
~Josh. 3:5 (KJV)

The use of the word *sanctify* in that verse is misleading since the New Testament clearly states that the Holy Ghost is responsible for any sanctifying work which takes place in the life of a believer. A better rendering of it would be,

"Then Joshua said to the people, "Consecrate yourselves, for tomorrow the Lord will do wonders among you.""
~Josh. 3:5

See the difference? Consecration is our job, and sanctification is that of the Spirit.

Before I continue, I need to provide a disclaimer of sorts.

It is possible for someone to consecrate another person, place, or thing for acts of holy service, other than themselves.

However, in order to do so, the person doing that has to have the authority to carry out such an act. And, the person, place, or thing has to be established through the act of consecration—for the service of consecration—by carrying out the things which validate the act itself. Once the person with authority has released consecration, they no longer bear the personal responsibility of bringing it to pass. That becomes the charge of others to fulfill. An example of that is found in Jer. 1:5 which says, *"Before I formed you in the womb I knew you, and before you were born I consecrated you; I have appointed you a prophet to the nations."* (NASB)

Here we see that Jehovah has done the consecrating. Thereafter, it is Joshua's task to walk it out. Said another way, God set Joshua apart, and it became his responsibility to carry that calling out.

There's another aspect of the process of consecration which has to do with how and when the process itself is to be carried out. I'll show you what I mean by opening up Josh. 3:5 a little, in order to see it from another angle than just the words of the page.

To catch the dynamic of what that verse says, it needs to be considered from an active real-time perspective:

Joshua tells the people to consecrate themselves based on what Jehovah is about to do in their midst. In other words, they are to prepare for what's about to happen prior to the event taking place. The best way to see that unfolding is to read the text like this:

"Consecrate yourselves [TODAY], for tomorrow the Lord will do wonders among you [TOMORROW]."

The act of consecration is to be addressed and set in motion before the need to serve becomes necessary. To not do so can result in missing the opportunity to be directly involved in what's going to take place, because the required setting apart hasn't happened.

I know this can get confusing to sort through, so I'll provide another example from a practical viewpoint to help you see what I'm saying.

Let's suppose I purpose to invite a few friends on an all-expenses-paid trip to somewhere wonderful. So, I have them all meet me for dinner where everyone covers their own meal. Before we finish to head home, I tell them about my surprise *gift*. After they all get over the shock of the news, I tell them there are just two things that they are required to do:

1. Go home and sort out time away from work and all their daily responsibilities.
2. Show up at the airport early enough to make certain they won't miss the flight.

Then I tell them that if they don't take care of point #1 it will likely make it impossible for them to join us. And, if they don't attend to point #2, those who are have checked in at the boarding gate will *leave without them*!

That, friend(s), is how the process of consecration is designed to work. You have to take care of everything that is needed for a set-apart life *before* any needs to participate begin to take place. If not, it is possible that you'll be aware that something wonderful is taking place. You may even be able to see it unfolding. However, you might not be able to take part in any part of the action. Why? Because you didn't consecrate yourself prior to the need for consecration to be in place.

Selah...pause and consider.

Now look at (meaning *read*) 2 Chron. 29 for a biblically-based scene to unfold regarding the consecration process. This is important to conveying this story: You'll need the entire chapter for context and outcome. However, I'll just focus on verses 31-36 with a brief overview.

The short version is presented in 2 Chron. 29:31-36 goes like this:

A service (celebration/holy convocation) was taking place. Due to unexpected circumstances, those who needed to be prepared to serve (the priests) had not consecrated themselves properly. However, the musicians who had come to serve in their capacity as musicians had, in fact, set themselves apart for holy service *before* their services were required. As a result, they were chosen to serve right in the very middle of the move of God, even though they weren't trained to operate in the role they found themselves in. What qualified them for the task at hand was not their training, nor their specific giftings. Rather, they were drafted into active service merely because they had come to the event already consecrated.

The principle contained in this story is truly amazing. At least it is to me. The ability to be used by God in a totally other way than the musicians had ever experienced took place simply because they showed up ready. The point, the focus, the intent of what I'm saying here is this: Consecration should be considered as a way of life for the followers of Christ. That is, if they want to be used of the Lord instead of merely hearing about some move of God, or perhaps even watching it unfold. To participate in what the Spirit is doing requires us to be ready before the *doing* ever begins.

That being the case, the first-time act of consecration which takes place should not be considered as the only time such an action is necessary. As believers, we should make it a pro-active goal to prayerfully set ourselves apart on a daily basis. In doing so, we will then be in a position to serve the will and way(s) of the God as He sees fit, based on His timing, and intention. (See 1 Pet. 2:9.)

*Worship is obedient service
manifesting through self-sacrifice.*

A Pondering
CONTENT AND CONTEXT

With this article, I'm targeting any and all so-called 5-Fold Ministry leaders (See Eph. 4:11-16). The subject matter could be of interest to other followers of Christ as well. But, the primary recipients are apostles, prophets, evangelists, pastors, and teachers. Those who the Lord continues to place in charge of helping to equip the body of Christ in order to serve the church-at-large and to help mature all the saints to serve. Those two specific tasks require the user-friendly ability of ministering the Word of God to the people in the pews. Remember pews?

Those who use the Bible as an essential and ongoing part of their public ministry should most assuredly do so with not only a deep level of sober-mindedness and sacred reverence, but also with an ability to "rightly divide" the Word (2 Tim. 2:15). With that in mind, I'm going to examine a way in which Scripture can be handled and processed in relationship to its content and its context.

To do so, I'll share a curious sort of revelation which the Holy Ghost gave me a couple of years ago while in ministry in Africa. It has served me (and others) well by providing an example of how both content and context are interrelated.

Here it is:

CONTENT and CONTEXT

Suppose you have a wallet, and it contains things which you keep there. The content of the wallet would be considered as being contained in the context of it. Next, take the wallet (including its content) and place it in a larger shoulder bag. As you place the wallet in the bag, be aware that bag has its own content in it. You would then have a wallet as a context, containing its own content, as well as a bag as a larger context, containing its own content. Both items would become the context for their own contents—but both of the contents would be in their own separate context. They would be together, yet separate. Now, repeat the process with a still larger container of some sort, large enough to hold the wallet (and its content), and the shoulder bag (and its content). Stay with me, I'm not finished...

Using that example, consider the Bible this way:

Each verse contains content. The content of each verse is placed in the context of a chapter. Then the content of each chapter is placed in the context of a specific book. Thereafter, each book (and its content) is placed in the context of the Bible. The entire counsel of God—from cover to cover. From there, only one step remains. Place the Bible (and all its contents) into the context of the Kingdom of God. That's exactly how I believe each and every aspect of Scripture is to be considered and applied. The Bible contains all the content necessary to live the kind of spiritual life humans were created to live. And, the Kingdom of God provides the context for all the contents to be pondered, appropriated, and practiced.

The Kingdom of God is *The Context* into which the content of all Scripture is to be procured, processed, and promoted. Without a proper Biblical context, everything we attempt to accomplish as Christians is at best random—having no fitting context for its content. I'm just sayin'...

A Pondering
SPIRITUAL RECALIBRATION

I was born again in 1955 when I was 9 years old. I grew up in the church till I was 15 or thereabouts. At that point I began to wander away from the fold of God. That's a term you rarely ever hear anymore. But, back in those daze it was mentioned a lot. So was the term "backslider," which is no longer used either. I became a prodigal for a decade and a half. Then in 1978, I came to the end of myself, having had a Ps. 38 experience.

> *[A poetic lament to remember, by King David]*
> *"O Lord, don't punish me angrily for what I've done. Don't let my sin inflame your wrath against me. For the arrows of your conviction have pierced me deeply. Your blows have struck my soul and crushed me. Now my body is sick. My health is totally broken because of your anger, and it's all due to my sins! I'm overwhelmed, swamped, and submerged beneath the heavy burden of my guilt. It clings to me and won't let me go. My rotting wounds are a witness against me. They are severe and getting worse, reminding me of my failure and folly. I am completely broken because of what I've done.*

Gloom is all around me. My sins have bent me over to the ground. My inner being is shriveled up; my self-confidence crushed. Sick with fever, I'm left exhausted. Now I'm cold as a corpse and nothing is left inside me but great groaning filled with anguish. Lord, you know all my desires and deepest longings. My tears are liquid words and you can read them all. My heart beats wildly, my strength is sapped, and the light of my eyes is going out. My friends stay far away from me, avoiding me like the plague. Even my family wants nothing to do with me. Meanwhile my enemies are out to kill me, plotting my ruin, speaking of my doom as they spend every waking moment planning how to finish me off. I'm like a deaf man who no longer hears. I can't even speak up, and words fail me; I have no argument to counter their threats. Lord, the only thing I can do is wait and put my hope in you. I wait for your help, my God. So hear my cry and put an end to their strutting in pride, who gloat when I stumble in pain. I'm slipping away and on the verge of a breakdown, with nothing but sorrow and sighing. I confess all my sin to you; I can't hold it in any longer. My agonizing thoughts punish me for my wrongdoing; I feel condemned as I consider all I've done. My enemies are many. They hate me and persecute me, though I've done nothing against them to deserve it. I show goodness to them and get repaid evil in return. And they hate me even more when I stand for what is right. So don't forsake me now, Lord! Don't leave me in this condition. God, hurry to help me, run to my rescue! For you're my Savior and my only hope!"

~Ps. 38 (TPT)

God had ordained circumstances which drew me back into

the fellowship of the saints and I rededicated my life to Christ and was baptized in the Spirit on the third Sunday night in May of that year. From then till now (some 41 years or so later), I have been pressing on to the mark of the high calling of the Lord (Phil. 3:14).

> *"I'm not saying that I have this all together, that I have it made. But I am well on my way, reaching out for Christ, who has so wondrously reached out for me. Friends, don't get me wrong: By no means do I count myself an expert in all of this, but I've got my eye on the goal, where God is beckoning us onward—to Jesus. I'm off and running, and I'm not turning back."*
>
> ~Phil. 3:14 (MSG)

In my early teens this was my grandmother's favorite song. I bought the sheet music and kept it in my guitar case from the day I bought it till I returned from my prodigal wanderings. I can't recall where it ended up. However, I've carried it in my heart for over 60 years. (See also 2 Tim. 1:12.)

I WAS THERE WHEN IT HAPPENED

There are some people who say we cannot tell
Whether we are saved or whether all is well
They say we only can hope and trust that it is so
Well, I was there when it happened and so I guess I ought to know

CHORUS:
Yes, I know when Jesus saved me (saved my soul)
The very moment He forgave me (made me whole)

SPIRITUAL RECALIBRATION

He took away my heavy burdens
Lord, He gave me peace within (peace within)
Satan can't make me doubt it (I won't doubt it)
It's real and I'm gonna shout it (I'm gonna shout it)
I was there when it happened
And so I guess I ought to know

I don't care who tells me salvation is not real
Though the world may argue, that we cannot feel
The heavy burden when it's lifted and the vile sin when it goes
(But) I was there when it happened and so I guess I ought to know

REPEAT CHORUS:
(Fern Jones, Peermusic Ltd, used by permission)

In March of 2018, I had a divine encounter with the Holy Ghost which has prompted me to reconsider, reevaluate, redefine, reboot, and recalibrate my spiritual life in a way most profound. I'll try and explain…

I'll cut to the chase here at the top and then work my way back to it.

"Seek first the Kingdom of God and His righteousness…"
~Mt. 6:33

If the most important person who has ever lived on earth said that was the charge given to all those who will follow Him, then it must certainly be Priority #1. If it isn't, then why is the word *first* in the text?

The encounter I mentioned above, the Divine one, has as its very foundation the principle of making certain that seeking

PARTICULAR PONDERING(S)

God's Kingdom is the first and foremost quest that I'll be pro-active about for the rest of my life. In order to pursue that goal, there are several things which should be factored into the sojourn:

Jesus is the embodiment of God's Kingdom—they are, or should be, linked together.

The Kingdom of God is eternal (with no beginning, middle, or ending). It was, is, and will be—eternally.

Being in the kingdom doesn't mean that you are active in it.

The Kingdom of God is *The Context* out of which each and every aspect of a spiritual life as a follower of Christ is intended to flow.

Without an understanding of, and direct involvement with God's Kingdom, a believer cannot fulfill the charge given to those who serve Christ based on 2 Cor. 5:18-21. We are to carry out the "ministry of reconciliation" (our job description) as "ambassadors for Christ" (our job title).

Representation of God's Kingdom here on earth as it is in heaven was modeled to us in the earthly life of Jesus. That is to say, how He lived out the obedient service that He offered up to reflect God's Kingdom is the way those who follow Him are to live as well. That is to say, His followers should follow Him I in modeling and representing Kingdom reality.

The start-up steps for activating the Kingdom of God are given in the Beatitudes (Mt. 5:1-12). The entire protocol for how the Kingdom is to operate is presented in the Sermon on the Mount (Mt. 5,6, and 7).

Each of those points could be a book in themselves. That's not my intention here. I'm only presenting them as pondering targets should you choose to unpack them for yourself.

Cause And Effect
REAPING AND SOWING

"If my *people, which are called by* my name, *shall humble themselves, and* pray, *and* seek *my face, and* turn *from their wicked ways;* then *will I hear from heaven, and will [forgive their sin], and will* heal their land."
~2 Chron. 7:14 (KJV, emphasis mine)

Humble: Strong's Concordance
To bend the knee; to bring low in subjection

In the text above, being humble is the first step in a series of things which those who are part of the Kingdom of God are charged with doing, in order to see a healing of their land take place. The series is: be humble, pray, seek, and turn. That process (according to the Word) then sets the stage for God to hear, forgive, and heal. His response is based on the obedient and yielded prompting(s) of His people.

FYI: That verse is directed to God's people, followers of Christ, born again believers. It is not addressed to any others who are not part of that specific people group.

"As you live this new life, we pray that you will be strengthened from God's boundless resources, so that you will find yourselves able to pass through any experience and endure it with courage. You will even be able to thank God in the midst of pain and distress because you are privileged to share the lot of those who are living in the light. For we must never forget that he rescued us from the power of darkness, and re-established us in the kingdom of his beloved Son, that is, in the kingdom of light. For it is by his Son alone that we have been redeemed and have had our sins forgiven."
~Col. 1:13–14 (Phillips)

Selah…pause and consider.

A Pondering
TO MY SPIRITUAL COHORTS

Becoming kingdom citizens took place when we were redeemed into Christ. In other words, our heavenly citizenship is a by-product of salvation. It is already accomplished—past tense.

> *"For He rescued us from the dominion of darkness, and transferred us to the kingdom of His beloved Son, in whom we have redemption, to forgiveness of sins."*
> ~Col. 1:13, emphasis mine

Therefore being "in Christ" and in God's kingdom, we also share in what Rev. 1:9 says, we are "partakers in the tribulation and kingdom and perseverance which are in Jesus..."

In light of that, we should take this to heart:

> *"Friends, when life gets really difficult, don't jump to the conclusion that God isn't on the job. Instead, be glad that you are in the very thick of what Christ experienced. This is a spiritual refining process, with glory just around the corner."*
> ~1 Pet. 4:12–13 (MSG)

A Pondering
PASTOR TO PASTURE

By the time this book goes to print I will have been retired for three years or thereabouts. During that time I've learned that there is a lot more to learn about retirement than I knew prior to crossing over into it. I do however have an observation or two to pass along. For the sake of historical documentation here goes.

1. If you have no personal history with retirement, any comments you make are likely incorrect, having not experienced the process yourself.
2. If any comments you make regarding retirement are based on what others have told you, they too are likely incorrect. Why? Because they are based on others' experiences rather than your own. Doing that is like trying to explain what marriage is like having never been married. Or like telling someone what child-rearing is like without ever having been a parent. Really, you can't get there from here.
3. In order to address retirement with any degree of substantive truth (proof), one first has to have some personal history with the process. But, the thing is, some "off

the clock" time has to first pass by (perhaps a few years) before any meaningful understanding begins to take shape. And, as one ages through the process, they can often become less concerned with trying to explain their point of view to anyone. Or, they simply forget, or find themselves too old to care or bother.

If you really want to know how I'm handling my retiring life, check back with me in another two or three years.

To be continued…

A Pondering
TRANSCENDING TRIBALISM

Tribalism: NOUN
The state or fact of being organized in a tribe or tribes.
The behavior and attitudes that stem from strong loyalty to one's own tribe or social group.

Humanity is being fractured on a global level by tribalism. Families, communities, regions, and nations are facing off at one another with a variance and divisiveness which makes the concept of unity virtually impossible. The depth and breadth of that reality goes far beyond my ability to effectively address it by offering a fix for humankind's disjointed condition. I can however present a model for those who consider themselves to be Christian in their beliefs, and how they're lived out. It's found in Scripture.

> "And God has made all things new, and reconciled us to himself, and given us the ministry of reconciling others to God. In other words, it was through the Anointed One that God was shepherding the world, not even keeping records of their transgressions, and he has entrusted to us the ministry of opening the door of reconciliation to God.

We are ambassadors of the Anointed One who carry the message of Christ to the world, *as though God were tenderly pleading with them directly through our lips. So we tenderly plead with you on Christ's behalf,* "Turn back to God and be reconciled to him." *For God made the only one who did not know sin to become sin for us, so that we who did not know righteousness might become the righteousness of God through our union with him."*

~2 Cor. 5:18-21 (TPT, emphasis mine)

Followers of Christ can only hope to carry out such a biblically-based charge by purposing to first accept what that text is saying, and then commit to becoming pro-active by implementing it in real time, and in real life—though the presence, power, and purpose of the Holy Spirit. I see no other way for unity to begin taking shape without God's people moving together, linked into such a mandate.

"How truly wonderful and delightful to see brothers and sisters living together in sweet unity! It's as precious as the sacred scented oil flowing from the head of the high priest Aaron, dripping down upon his beard and running all the way down to the hem of his priestly robes. This heavenly harmony can be compared to the dew dripping down from the skies upon Mount Hermon, refreshing the mountain slopes of Israel. For from this realm of sweet harmony God will release his eternal blessing, the promise of life forever!"

~Ps. 133 (TPT)

There's another passage which speaks directly to how an individual can begin putting the "ministry of reconciliation" and their "ambassadorship for Christ" together in a pro-active manner.

> *"With what shall I come before the Lord, and bow myself before God on high?*
>
> *Shall I come before him with burnt offerings, with calves a year old? Will the Lord be pleased with thousands of rams, with ten thousands of rivers of oil?*
>
> *Shall I give my firstborn for my transgression, the fruit of my body for the sin of my soul? He has told you, O man, what is good; and what does the Lord require of you but to do justice, and to love kindness, and to walk humbly with your God?"*
>
> ~Micah 6:6-8 (ESV)

I'll include an alternate rendering because I like the picture it presents.

> *"How can I stand up before God and show proper respect to the high God?*
>
> *Should I bring an armload of offerings topped off with yearling calves?*
>
> *Would God be impressed with thousands of rams, with buckets and barrels of olive oil? Would he be moved if I sacrificed my firstborn child, my precious baby, to cancel my sin? But he's already made it plain how to live, what to do, what God is looking for in men and women.*
>
> *It's quite simple: Do what is fair and just to your neighbor, be compassionate and loyal in your love, and don't take yourself too seriously—take God seriously."*
>
> ~Micah 6:6-8 (MSG)

The directive in that passage points to three things in specific which are required (on a personal level) in order to position oneself as a unifier rather than a divider. Keep in mind that the process of implementing reconciliation is not to birth some sort of grand movement. Such a reformation must be approached on a person-to-person basis. If a wide-reaching movement is to take shape, it can only happen as individuals begin to apply the principles and precepts of what the Scriptural passages I've included in this drafting encourage.

Do justice: To do justice is to learn it, embrace it, and then live it out in daily life.

Love kindness: To love kindness is to respond to it emotionally, mentally, and spiritually. It is, in essence, participation in the so-called Golden Rule.

"Here is a simple, rule-of-thumb guide for behavior: Ask yourself what you want people to do for you, then grab the initiative and do it for them. Add up God's Law and Prophets and this is what you get."

~Mt. 7:12-14 (MSG)

Walk humbly: To walk humbly with your God is first and foremost a sign of yielded obedience to the Sovereign that you serve. For Christians, exactly who that is can be answered simply with only one verse from the Bible.

"Thou shall have no other gods *before Me."

~Deut. 5:7

*The NASB uses the word *besides* instead of *before*. I prefer that image. It's much broader and distinctive in its scope and application.

PARTICULAR PONDERING(S)

My intention here isn't to debate, dissuade, criticize, or condemn other forms or aspects of religion. I am personally a follower of Christ, a born again believer, and a citizen of God's eternal kingdom (1 Pet. 2:9). I serve the King of kings, Christ Jesus, the Lord of lords. My position in regards to what I'm stating in this narrative—and throughout this entire book—is this:

> *"...Fear God. Worship him in total commitment. Get rid of the gods your ancestors worshiped on the far side of The River (the Euphrates) and in Egypt. You, worship God. "If you decide that it's a bad thing to worship God, then choose a god you'd rather serve—and do it today. Choose one of the gods your ancestors worshiped from the country beyond The River, or one of the gods of the Amorites, on whose land you're now living. As for me and my family, we'll worship God."*
> ~Josh. 24:14–15 (MSG)

UNITY
(Ps.133)

Behold how good and pleasant it is
When believers are gathered in unity
It's like the dew of Hermon
Coming down on Mt. Zion
Where the people of God see their destiny

There the Lord commands a blessing
When He hears us all rejoicing
In the bond that's been created
Through the blood of our Redeemer

CHORUS:
He gives us life forevermore
Life forevermore
Life forevermore
When we are united in Him

Behold how good and pleasant it is
To be seated with God in the heavenlies
It like the dew of Hermon
Coming down on Mt. Zion
And washing away our iniquity

REPEAT CHORUS:

(W. Berry / See & Say Songs, BMI)

A Pondering
STILL STANDING

"Having done all, stand."

~Eph. 6:13

"On Christ the solid rock I stand…"

~Edward Mote ,1834

The lyrics below were birthed from one of the most overlooked and most precious verses in God's Word to me. Consider it in light of what Paul says in 2 Cor. 4:17–18 and you'll find yourself drinking from deep well(s) of salvation, hope and encouragement. (Isa. 12:2–3)

> *"For this light momentary affliction is preparing for us an eternal weight of glory beyond all comparison, 18 as we look not to the things that are seen but to the things that are unseen. For the things that are seen are transient, but the things that are unseen are eternal."*
>
> ~2 Cor. 4:17–18 (ESV)

> *Behold, God is my salvation; "I will trust, and will not be*

afraid; for the Lord God is my strength and my song, and he has become my salvation. With joy you will draw water from the wells of salvation."

~Isa.12:2–3 (ESV)

BEAUTIFUL
(2 Cor. 4:17)

*The winds of change keep blowin',
just like they always do
Testing our foundation,
of what we'll accept as true
Those who build their lives on Jesus,
have nothing they should fear
The storms may come a rumblin',
but in Christ they'll persevere*
CHORUS:
*When He sees us standing, standing in the Son
It fills His heart with gladness, at the good work that's begun
When He sees us standing, standing in the Son
We're beautiful, we're beautiful in His eyes*

*The hope that fills tomorrow
Is the dream we've yet to see
It's the coming of The Kingdom,
where we'll live eternally
The faith that keeps us goin',
is a gift from up above
Provision from our Maker,
as a token of His love*
REPEAT CHORUS:

PARTICULAR PONDERING(S)

BRIDGE:
He sees us as completed, He sees us as perfected
He sees us through His Holy Son, chosen and accepted
He sees us as a priesthood, set apart for His alone
He sees us in eternity in worship 'round His throne
REPEAT CHORUS:
(W. Berry / See & Say Songs, BMI)

That song is personal, corporate, and prophetic in content and intent. Personal because it manifested out of my heart directly to the Father, Son, and Holy Ghost as a worship offering (Rom. 12:1–2). Corporate because it can be sung (embraced) by any and all who are *"hidden with Christ in God"* (Col. 3:1-3). And prophetic because it speaks of what's yet to come. (see Col. 1:13 / 1 Pet. 2:9).

"Oh, dear children of mine (forgive the affection of an old man!), have you realized it? Here and now we are God's children. We don't know what we shall become in the future. We only know that, if reality were to break through, we should reflect his likeness, for we should see him as he really is!"
~1 Jn. 3:2 (Phillips)

"For the grace of God, which can save every man, has now become known, and it teaches us to have no more to do with godlessness or the desires of this world but to live, here and now, responsible, honorable and God-fearing lives. And while we live this life we hope and wait for the glorious pronouncement of the Great God and of Jesus Christ our Savior. For he gave himself for us all, that he might rescue us from all our evil ways and make for himself a people of his own, clean and

pure, with our hearts set upon living a life that is good."
~Titus 2:13–14 (Phillips)

"Looking for that Blessed Hope, *and the glorious appearing of the great God and our Savior Jesus Christ…"*
~Titus 2:13 (KJV, emphasis mine)

"I need to emphasize, friends, that our natural, earthy lives don't in themselves lead us by their very nature into the kingdom of God. Their very "nature" is to die, so how could they "naturally" end up in the Life kingdom? But let me tell you something wonderful, a mystery I'll probably never fully understand. We're not all going to die—but we are all going to be changed. You hear a blast to end all blasts from a trumpet, and in the time that you look up and blink your eyes—it's over. On signal from that trumpet from heaven, the dead will be up and out of their graves, beyond the reach of death, never to die again. At the same moment and in the same way, we'll all be changed. In the resurrection scheme of things, this has to happen: everything perishable taken off the shelves and replaced by the imperishable, this mortal replaced by the immortal. Then the saying will come true:

Death swallowed by triumphant Life!
Who got the last word, oh, Death?
Oh, Death, who's afraid of you now?

It was sin that made death so frightening and law-code guilt that gave sin its leverage, its destructive power. But now in a single victorious stroke of Life, all three—sin, guilt, death—are gone, the gift of our Master, Jesus Christ. Thank God!"
~1 Cor. 15:50-57 (MSG)

PARTICULAR PONDERING(S)

Those who have received Christ Jesus as their personal Savior are, in fact, beautiful in His eyes.

Amen. So be it. I'm down with that.

A Biblical Perspective
OBSERVATIONAL IMPLICATIONS

> *"So now: Fear God. Worship him in total commitment. Get rid of the gods your ancestors worshiped on the far side of The River (the Euphrates) and in Egypt. You, worship God. If you decide that it's a bad thing to worship God, then choose a god you'd rather serve—and do it today. Choose one of the gods your ancestors worshiped from the country beyond The River, or one of the gods of the Amorites, on whose land you're now living. As for me and my family, we'll worship God."*
> ~Josh. 24:14-24 (MSG)

Notice that Joshua didn't make his position known by attempting in any way to discredit, demean, dismiss, or diminish anyone else's religious convictions—or the lack thereof. Nope, he did not. Instead he declared his position by making it clear who he had put his hope, faith, and trust in. It saddens me deeply that a vast number of those who follow Christ today no longer apply Joshua's testimonial model directly to their own.

Scripture says clearly that vindication comes from the Lord.

PARTICULAR PONDERING(S)

Our job is not to push our own agenda—or God's either for that matter. Our calling is to represent His Sovereign Kingdom here on earth as it is in heaven (Mt. 6:9-13). Scripture charges us to do that by offering the "ministry of reconciliation" (our job description) while serving as "ambassadors for Christ" (our job title). If those who are redeemed of the Lord were to faithfully put 2 Cor. 5:18-21 into practice, the expansion and fulfillment of the so-called Great Commission would likely begin to unfold on a truly profound and unprecedented historical level.

> *"…and the earth will be filled with the knowledge of the glory of God as the waters cover the sea."*
> ~Hab. 2:14 (See also Deut. 5:7)

> *"Let the peace of Christ keep you in tune with each other, in step with each other. None of this going off and doing your own thing. And cultivate thankfulness. Let the Word of Christ—the Message—have the run of the house. Give it plenty of room in your lives. Instruct and direct one another using good common sense. And sing, sing your hearts out to God! Let every detail in your lives—words, actions, whatever—be done in the name of the Master, Jesus, thanking God the Father every step of the way."*
> ~Col. 3:17 (MSG)

Spiritual Recalibration
HUMBLED PRAYER

> *"If My people who are called by My name will humble themselves, and pray and seek My face, and turn from their wicked ways, then I will hear from heaven, and will forgive their sin and heal their land."*
>
> ~2 Chron. 7:14 (NKJV)

According to the text above, the result of following the pathway from humility to prayer, to seeking God's face, and turning from wickedness is that God will hear us, forgive us, and heal our land.

Step #1 is humility.

Humble: To bend the knee; hence to humiliate, vanquish. To bring down (low), into subjection; to subdue. (Strong's Concordance)

> *"The sacrifices of God are a broken spirit; a* broken *and a* contrite *heart, O God, You will not despise."*
>
> Ps. 51:17 (emphasis mine)

Broken: To burst; to break (down, off, in pieces, up); to be brokenhearted; to bring to birth, crush, destroy, hurt, quench. (Strong's Concordance)

Contrite: To collapse (physically or mentally); to break or cause to crouch. (Strong's Concordance)

Implementing Step #1:

> *"Be careful (*anxious / NASB*) for nothing; but in everything by* prayer *and* supplication *with thanksgiving let your requests be made known unto God.*
> ~Phil. 4:6 (KJV emphasis mine)

To continue from the text above—

Prayer: Worship. From a word meaning to come alongside God through supplication (Strong's Concordance)

Supplication: To petition or request. From a word meaning to beg (as binding oneself).

If followers of Christ aren't pro-active in this process, then why would we think that God is bound to be pro-active in regards to doing His part—healing our land? Kingdom citizens (1 Pet. 2:9) are charged with humbling ourselves (1 Pet. 5:6), seeking God's face, and turning from our wicked ways. God's response is based on ours.

Selah…pause and consider.

Putting the passage above into practice requires several Biblically-based principles, including patient endurance, ongoing forgiveness, and learning how to live out the "ministry of reconciliation" (2 Cor. 5:19) which says, *"God was in Christ reconciling the world to himself, not counting their trespasses against them…"* None of that is possible without the help of the Holy

Ghost—the Sanctifier of all those who are followers of Christ (2 Thess. 2:13 and 1 Pet. 1:2) . Just sayin'.

A Pondering
COMBATING THE GLOBAL PANDEMIC OF LONELINESS

Loneliness is a by-product of hopelessness. When hope diminishes, loneliness often increases. And if loneliness shows up, it can bring oppression with it. That in turn may led to depression resulting in a clustered-combination of other physical, psychological, and spiritual issues. Scripturally speaking, Paul had this to say (as a disciple of Jesus) when addressing those who were purposed to live as followers of Christ.

> *"If in Christ we have hope in this life only, we are of all people most to be pitied."*
> ~1 Cor. 15:19 (ESV)

Not only does hopelessness manifest as loneliness, it also restricts the ability to live and walk / by and in faith.

> "Faith *is the substance of things* hoped *for,* the evidence of things not seen."
> ~Heb. 11:1, emphasis mine

In order to be able to function with active faith in life, hope must first be resident. And, for hope to be present (indwelling), it must come from somewhere.

> *"May the Lord Jesus Christ and God our Father (who has loved us and given us unending encouragement and unfailing hope by his grace) inspire you with courage and confidence in every good thing you say or do."*
> ~2 Thess. 2:16-17 (Phillips)

As the source of hope, grace flows from the throne of grace directly into a heart willing to request it and receive it.

> *"Let us then with confidence draw near to the throne of grace, that we may receive mercy and find grace to help in time of need.*
> ~Heb. 4:16 (ESV)

Thereafter hope produces the manifesting evidence of faith, which in turn enables a lifestyle that can overcome (combat) loneliness, resulting in the acquisition of righteousness, peace, and joy as citizens in the kingdom of God (See Rom. 14:17; Col.1:13; 2 Pet. 2:9).

Inheritance
A PLACE TO STAND

Scripture tells us what Paul's ministry was meant to do when he was called and sent forth. His charge was to the Gentiles which was everyone who wasn't Jewish by birth or practicing their religious belief.

> *"I send you to open their eyes, to turn them from darkness to light, from the power of Satan to God himself, so that they may know forgiveness of their sins and take their *place with all those who are made holy by their faith in me."*
> ~Acts 26:18 (Phillips)

*Inheritance (KJV) Heirship; a possession. From a word meaning of partitioning (a sharer by lot). An heir.

The place (or inheritance) those who follow Christ have been given is expressed here:

> *"As you live this new life, we pray that you will be strengthened from God's boundless resources, so that you will find yourselves able to pass through any experience and endure it with courage. You will even be able to thank God in the*

midst of pain and distress because you are privileged to share the lot of those who are living in the light. For we must never forget that he rescued us from the power of darkness, and re-established us in the kingdom of his beloved Son, that is, in the kingdom of light. For it is by his Son alone that we have been redeemed and have had our sins forgiven."

~Col. 1:13 (Phillips)

"But you are God's "chosen generation", his "royal priesthood", his "holy nation", his "peculiar people"—all the old titles of God's people now belong to you. It is for you now to demonstrate the goodness of him who has called you out of darkness into his amazing light. In the past you were not "a people" at all: now you are the people of God. In the past you had no experience of his mercy, but now it is intimately yours."

~1 Pet. 2:9 (Phillips)

Sanctification
KINGDOM DYNAMICS

A little over 42 years ago I fell under deep conviction regarding my dented and damaged spiritual relationship with the Father, Son, and Holy Ghost. Having lived as a prodigal for some 15+ years, I was being drawn back into the fold of God, and the fellowship of the saints (the body of Christ).

The Process: Conviction to Confession to Repentance to Restoration and Renewal

During an eight-month period, the Spirit kept impressing on my mind and penetrating my heart with two directives:
1. Pay attention
2. Practice patience

Now, four plus decades later, and approaching my 74th birthday, I am still sorting out the implications of those two things. They both seem timely in these daze we're all finding ourselves in currently.

Looking at Language
SORRY VS. FORGIVENESS

There is a distinction between saying you're sorry and asking for forgiveness. Consider this: When we say we're sorry, we are retaining a degree of personal control. Even though we may be sincere in our apology, and saddened by what we've done, the request is based on our action. Whereas asking for forgiveness shifts the control from us to the person (or group) that has been offended, wounded, or disparaged. By submitting (giving over) the transaction to the one who has been violated, you are affording them the opportunity to be reconciled to you and you to them on their terms.

To clarify: Saying you're sorry isn't wrong as such. It's just that it doesn't go deep enough from a Biblical perspective. It leaves some portion of you in the interchange. The better (or fitting) response in relationship to brokenness and contrition is to place the control regarding resolution with someone other than ourselves. (See Ps. 51 and note verse 17)

One more thing: Repentance doesn't mean that you're sorry. Scripturally speaking it means to change the way you think; to turn around or away from; to go in a different direction.

A Pondering
HOPE FOR HOPE

"If in Christ we have hope in this life only, we are of all people most to be pitied."

~1 Cor. 15:19 (ESV)

That verse was written by a believer to believers. In essence, it's intent is to inform those who follow Christ that hope (eternal-kingdom-based-hope) is very important. Here's why: People cannot live by faith unless/until hope is first resident in their lives.

"Now faith is the substance *of things* hoped *for, the* evidence *of things not seen.*

Heb. 11:1 (KJV, emphasis mine)

If hope is first required in order for faith to manifest, then where do we acquire hope? Scripture says that it comes through the flow of grace into our spiritual reservoirs.

"Now may our Lord Jesus Christ himself, and God our Father,

who loved us and gave us eternal comfort and good hope through grace, *comfort your hearts and establish them in every good work and word."*

~2 Thess. 2:16-17 / ESV, emphasis mine)

If it takes grace to channel grace into those hope tanks, then where do we get it—where is such grace found? Again, Scripture provides the answer:

"Let us then with confidence draw near *to the* throne of grace, *that we may* receive mercy and find grace *to help in time of need."*

~Heb. 4:16 (ESV, emphasis mine)

The verse presents us with two dynamic aspects which are to be considered when seeking for ongoing, daily, fresh grace:
1. We are to go boldly before the throne of grace and solicit (request) it
2. We are to secure it (along with mercy), for ourselves and also for others to provide help in time(s) of need – ours and/or theirs

If this were to be outworked as a mathematical equation, it would look like this: Grace + hope = faith

Now, do the math…

A Biblical Perspective
PLANS & PURPOSES

"Listen, those of you who are boasting, "Today or tomorrow we'll go to another city and spend some time and go into business and make heaps of profit!" But you don't have a clue what tomorrow may bring. For your fleeting life is but a warm breath of air that is visible in the cold only for a moment and then vanishes! Instead you should say, "Our tomorrows are in the Lord's hands and if he is willing we will live life to its fullest and do this or that." But here you are, boasting in your ignorance, for to be presumptuous about what you'll do tomorrow is evil! So if you know of an opportunity to do the right thing today, yet you refrain from doing it, you're guilty of sin."

~Ja. 4:13-17 (TPT)

That passage doesn't say we shouldn't make plans for the future. Of course not. It does however present a qualifying directive for those who consider themselves to be followers of Christ (Acts 4:12) ; ministers of reconciliation (2 Cor. 5:18-19); ambassadors for Christ (2 Cor. 5:20); and citizens of heaven (Col. 1:13, 1 Pet. 1:9). It states that factoring in God's sovereignty in regards to such matters as life, destiny, and the future should always be the major component in our plans and purposes.

I'll just leave this here…

See also Mt. 6:33

A Common Call to Contrition
THE PRINCIPLE OF BIBLICAL HUMALIATION

I will attempt to choose my words very carefully so as not to be misunderstood: Currently this is what the Holy Ghost has given me regarding what's taking place on the planet in terms of the pandemic and its pervasive impact on humanity....

As of this posting, there are at least 184 nations experiencing the stark dynamics of this global catastrophe. Aside from all the obvious similarities being addressed, there is one specific thing which is becoming a common denominator for everyone involved. Our collective cultural differences are being leveled (or brought down) from our high positions of self-will, self-rule, and self-determination. Humanity is being humbled by something unseen which we have no control over, and no clear course of prevention from or cure of.

DISCLAIMER: I'm not commenting on why this is happening, or how it has come to be. I have no idea as to either in that regard. They are (to me) mysteries. Such things are beyond my understanding (See Ps. 131). I am merely stating what I am discerning by listening to what the Spirit is telling me.

Self-help is not the remedy for this chaos, regardless of its source. But, brokenness, contrition, and humility may be. And likely repentance. (See Ps. 51)

We may be "in this together", but we are not in charge.

A Pondering
WORSHIP IN SPECIFIC

So here's what I want you to do, God helping you: Take your everyday, ordinary life—your sleeping, eating, going-to-work, and walking-around life—and place it before God as an offering. Embracing what God does for you is the best thing you can do for him. Don't become so well-adjusted to your culture that you fit into it without even thinking. Instead, fix your attention on God. You'll be changed from the inside out. Readily recognize what he wants from you, and quickly respond to it. Unlike the culture around you, always dragging you down to its level of immaturity, God brings the best out of you, develops well-formed maturity in you.
~Rom. 12:1–2 (MSG)

"God is seeking worshipers who will worship Him in spirit and in truth."
~Jn. 4:24

Those who worship Him (in specific) are in fact the kind of worshipers He seeks. How our worship manifest then becomes a natural flow out of our lives as living sacrifices.

Selah…pause and consider.

A Pondering
SCRIPTURAL OBEDIENCE

"If my people who are called by my name humble themselves, and pray and seek my face and turn from their wicked ways, then I will hear from heaven and will forgive their sin and heal their land.
~2 Chron. 7:14 (ESV)

That verse is getting a lot of digital air time currently. I'd imagine it's being read, spoken, pondered and prayed much more than it has been in a very long time. That being the case, let's unpack some of it together for a few moments.

I only want to consider the very first portion of the text for now, the "if My people who are called by My name" phrase. Why only that? Because it provides the *context* out of which the rest of the verse is to take place.

Here's what I mean: The directives in the verse are addressed to a very specifically defined group of people—those who consider themselves to be Jehovah's people (The Sovereign-Creator-God's people). The ones who are called (or known) by

His name. That is to say it is not meant as a directive to any other people who don't fit into those two clearly stated groups of human beings.

Selah…pause and consider.

It is not a charge given to world leaders; governmental bodies; law makers; court systems; cultural movers and shakers; social media influencers; spiritual lone-rangers; faithless-nay-sayers; super stars (performers/actors/athletes and such); denominational affiliates; so called religious theologians; scientists; pagans; non-believers; heathens; atheists; agnostics; etc., etc. etc. Nope. *It is addressed to god's people—period!*

With that in mind, consider this: While Jesus was hear on earth, He was the most knowledgeable being of God's will, God's way(s), and God's Word. He still is. That is to say, His theology was rock solid. Even when challenged it was unshakable. He knew the Old Testament writings better than anyone, ever. So His perspective regarding the verse under consideration here would have been spot on if He has chosen to comment on it. That would also have been true of any passage found anywhere in all of the sacred rite contained in the ancient scrolls.

So, when Jesus gave a word of direction to those who considered themselves followers of His, He was in a very real sense addressing the same people who were given the directive of 2 Chron. 7:14—God's people. However, He chose to give His disciples what He determined to be the first priority they should live by. Out of all the principles, precepts, laws, rules, status, ordinances; commandments and such presented in the Old Testament which He could have put forth as direction, He said this:

SCRIPTURAL OBEDIENCE

"...seek first the kingdom of God, and His righteousness..."
~Mt. 6:33

That being said, if you are, in fact, a child of God; chosen and elected; a citizen of heaven; a born again believer (1 Pet. 2:9), what is priority #1 in your life—right now, today, at this very moment?

Sanctification
AN ETERNAL PERSPECTIVE IN A TEMPORAL WORLD

Things which are eternal are—eternal, everlasting. They were, are, and will be—eternally. Things that are temporal are framed by earth-time. Sooner or later they'll come to an end. Followers of Christ should be giving way more attention and consideration to the difference between those two dynamic polarity points.

> "So if you're serious about living this new resurrection life with Christ, act like it. Pursue the things over which Christ presides. Don't shuffle along, eyes to the ground, absorbed with the things right in front of you. Look up, and be alert to what is going on around Christ—that's where the action is. See things from his perspective. Your old life is dead. Your new life, which is your real life—even though invisible to spectators—is with Christ in God. He is your life. When Christ (your real life, remember) shows up again on this earth, you'll show up, too—the real you, the glorious you. Meanwhile, be content with obscurity, like Christ."
> ~Col. 3:1-4 (MSG)

AN ETERNAL PERSPECTIVE IN A TEMPORAL WORLD

"In the dime stores and bus stations
People talk of situations
Read books, repeat quotations
Draw conclusions on the wall…"

B. Dylan

"A book must be the axe for the frozen sea within us."
~Kafka

"How you spend your days is how you spend your life."
~Annie Dillard

"See [life] for the fathomless mystery that it is. In the boredom and pain of it no less than in the excitement and gladness: touch, taste, smell your way to the holy and hidden heart of it because in the last analysis all moments are key moments, and life itself is grace."
~Frederick Buechner

PARTICULAR PONDERING(S)

ETERNITY'S WHISPER
(Ecc. 3:11)

In the first grey light of morning, in the fields of Alabama
A red-clay farmer bows his head, as he hears eternity's whisper
His works a daily struggle, he's barely breaking even
He longs to know the blessed rest God's promised 'round His throne

In the mid-day sun of L.A., on the sidewalks of the city
Some street-wise Angelino child here's eternity's whisper
His days are dark and desperate, he knows there's something better
The gospel of the kingdom may be all the proof he needs

CHORUS:
Can you hear eternity's whisper, listen
Can you hear eternity's whisper, listen, be still

BRIDGE:
Eternity's been set within the heart of everyman
Only those who hear God's call, truly understand

REPEAT CHORUS:

In the moments beyond midnight, down the alleys of Calcutta
The destitute and dying ones, hear eternity's whisper
And though I don't understand it, I know God's ways are perfect
So I have placed my hope upon His never-ending love

REPEAT CHORUS:
(W. Berry & M. McCall / See & Say Songs, BMI)

If You're Interested
PREVIOUS PROJECTS
(From back in the daze)

The link below will get you to all of my on line recorded audio and video products from back in the daze. Along with that, you'll also find a few songs of mine recorded by other artists.

Funding resources from all sales goes directly toward mission sojourning on the African continent through OUTBOUND MINISTRIES INTERNATIONAL.

For more information visit:

https://www.facebook.com/seeandsaysongs

Also Available From
WAYNE BERRY

Pondering(s)
Ponderings (Too)

Home at Last
Detour (A Prodigal's Chronicles)
Journey Mercies
with The Verge Band and Cohorts Caravan

Also Available From
WORDCRAFTS PRESS

Finding God in the Bathroom
by Rev. Brian C. Johnson, PhD

I Wish Someone Had Told Me
by Barbie Loflin

Donkey Tales
by Keith Alexis

I Am
by Summer McKinney

www.wordcrafts.net